*Yale Studies in English*, 193

# William Carlos Williams
## and the
## Meanings of Measure

*Stephen Cushman*

YALE UNIVERSITY PRESS
New Haven and London

Published with assistance from the Kingsley Trust Association Publication Fund
established by the Scroll and Key Society of Yale College.

Designed by Margaret E.B. Joyner
and set in Janson type
by Rainsford Type.
Printed in the United States of America
by BookCrafters, Inc., Chelsea, Michigan.

Library of Congress Cataloging in Publication Data

Cushman, Stephen, 1956–
  William Carlos Williams and the meanings of measure.

  (Yale studies in English; 193)
  Bibliography: p.
  Includes index.
  1. Williams, William Carlos, 1883–1963—Criticism
and interpretation.   2. Free verse.   3. Poetics.
I. Title.   II. Series.
PS3545.I544Z584     1985     811'.52     85–3364
ISBN 0–300–03373–7 (alk. paper)

The paper in this book meets the guidelines for permanence
and durability of the Committee on Production Guidelines
for Book Longevity of the Council on Library Resources.

10   9   8   7   6   5   4   3   2   1

*Credits appear on p. 161.*

For Sandy

# CONTENTS

# ACKNOWLEDGMENTS

I am indebted deeply to Thomas R. Whitaker and John Hollander for their teaching, their writing, and their guidance. To Marie Borroff, Louis Martz, the Committee on Yale Studies in English, and an anonymous reader I owe thanks for their close reading and their suggestions for revision. For their help with manuscript research, I am grateful to David E. Schoonover, curator, and the staff of the Collection of American Literature, Beinecke Rare Book and Manuscript Library, Yale University, as well as Robert J. Bertholf, curator, and the staff of the Poetry and Rare Books Collection of the Lockwood Memorial Library, State University of New York at Buffalo. While the manuscript, typed by Ruth Estep and Barbara Smith, was nearing its final form, a grant for summer research from the University of Virginia helped greatly. At Yale University Press Ellen Graham has been especially generous with her supply of patience, firmness, and encouragement. Thanks are due also to Cynthia Baughman, who edited the manuscript, and to John Lynch, who helped check and index the finished product. Finally, from friends, family, and my wife Sandy, I have received that which no acknowledgment touches.

# No Verse Is Free

But if by "too much freedom" they mean that
a man binds himself by ignoring the truths that
he cannot escape, no matter how hard he may
run, then I will listen.

—"America, Whitman, and the Art of Poetry"

Beginning with his essay "Speech Rhythm" (1913) in which he declares "time, not the syllables, *must* be counted,"[1] Williams crusaded on behalf of his theory of measure for nearly fifty years. During that time, a period which extends from the infancy of modernism to the emergence of the contemporary poetic generation, his theory of measure grew beyond prosody into mythology. For Williams measure became the Supreme Fiction, the all-embracing truth which is always a little more, or less, than truth. Like Stevens, who in one letter would declare the Supreme Fiction to be poetry and in another deny it,[2] Williams found himself and his theory haunted by contradictions. The larger measure grew, the harder it became to define. Was it primarily auditory, or was it also visual? Could it be counted, or simply felt? Did it approximate quantitative meter or musical time, or did it define some other kind of meter or time? Faced with such questions and inconsistencies, many of Williams's readers and critics have had to lead double lives, admiring his poems while apologizing for his theory. Those well-meaning readers who have set out determined not to apologize, but rather to explain, have found themselves hypnotized by Williams's logic and terminology, until soon they are solemnly repeating his slogans and formulations. Read-

ers who admire Williams's poetry, but who want neither to apologize
nor to explain, have the option of pretending that his theorizing does
not matter because, however flawed it may be, it cannot diminish
his poems.

But Williams's theory of measure does matter; it matters, if not
for what it tells at every moment about the prosody of nonmetrical
verse, then for what it tells about William Carlos Williams and the
mind behind his verse. The bifurcation of measure, into on the one
hand a prosodic concept and on the other a larger metaphor, reflects
a duality both in poetic form and in Williams's conception of poetic
form. Although Williams may well have been unaware of it, he
himself points to this duality in a letter to Cid Corman, written
August 11, 1958: "I use the word 'measure' in the original sense 'to
mete,' as the English used it at the beginning." Having quoted this
statement, Paul Mariani glosses it to mean that Williams is using
the word "in its sense of measuring *out*, which implied—obviously—
a standard against which to measure."[3] Still, obvious as this may
be, there is more to it.

Coming in 1958, Williams's statement to Corman carries the
authority of a poet reviewing his life's work and summarizing it; yet
here that summary oversimplifies. Williams did not use the word
"measure" consistently in any one sense. Before it became his ideological password, "measure" often carried neutral or even pejorative
connotations. In some contexts its meaning is specific and technical,
in others general and figurative. In appealing to etymology for clar-
ification, Williams implicitly acknowledges to Corman that ambiguity threatens his terminology. Williams himself, however, is not
solely responsible for that ambiguity. As he would have discovered
had he pressed further, or as he might have known but did not
explain to Corman, the etymology of "measure" is itself split. Descending through one Indo-European root (*mē-*), "measure" traces
its ancestry to the Greek *metron* ("a means of measuring"), which
gives the word "meter" and the specific, technical meanings of "measure" as a unit of poetic or musical composition; yet through a variant
of the same root (*med-*), we inherit a number of words having the
general meaning "to take appropriate measures." This is the etymological family Williams cites to Corman. This variant group gives
not only the archaic "to mete" (Old English *metan*), but also "meet"

(in the sense of commensurate, fitting, or appropriate), "meditate" (to measure something with thought), and—appropriately enough— "medicine" (from Latin *medicus*, a physician, one who measures man's ills and injuries). Clearly, the general, figurative meanings of measure come to Williams from this direction.

In turning to etymology, Williams is not merely showing off or playing the pedant; he is revealing a mental habit he inherits through the American tradition from Emerson, Whitman, Thoreau, and Melville, all of whom saw in etymology a means of recuperating the original poetic power of a modern language in ruins. Furthermore, in this particular case etymology reveals not only the origin of Williams's terminological confusion, and thus ours; it also reveals a doubleness in his conception of poetic form. This double vision does not necessarily represent a defect in Williams's thinking; rather, it reflects the rhetorical distinction between scheme and trope.[4] The construction of verse involves scheme, or the surface patterning and design of words, whereas the creation of poetry involves trope, or the discovery and presentation of nonliteral figures of meaning. When Williams uses "measure" in a specific, technical sense to signify pseudo-musical divisions in verse, he is discussing formal scheme. When he tells Corman that "measure" means "to mete," he is generating poetic trope. That the two uses of "measure" should blend into one another is inevitable, and perhaps even desirable, because such blending gives this term the peculiarly deep resonance of which poetic fictions and mythologies are made:

> I don't pretend that I know all the answers—but that the poetic measure must be to take its part among other measures in the assemblies of the age broken away from its ankylosed conditions I venture to dedicate myself, completely. We cannot escape it as intelligent men.[5]

Appearing in a late, fragmentary essay edited by Hugh Kenner and published in 1959, this statement exemplifies Williams's unmistakable tone and idiom. The opening disclaimer, "I don't pretend that I know all the answers," both confides and conceals, as Williams admits the limits of his knowledge, limits others, such as Pound and Eliot, often made him feel keenly; yet at the same time he neatly shields that knowledge from academic scrutiny which might be too exacting and from interpretations which might be too literal. In one of the better early studies of Williams's notion of measure, A. Kingsley Weatherhead cautions that this poet must be defended "from his own gossipy, off-the-cuff dicta on the subject, in letters, lectures, and essays, which may not be taken literally and accurately."[6] Although this warning serves as a needed corrective to arguments built solely on triumphant demonstrations that Williams's critical statements contradict themselves, it also underestimates the value of such statements. Weatherhead continues: "His prose is, to a great extent, hit or miss." Some of Williams's statements may hit and some may miss, but Williams was shrewder and his statements on measure more suggestive than Weatherhead seems to recognize. As in the quotation above, Williams often dissembles when he confesses. Having sidestepped a full-dress debate with a modest, disarming concession, he plows straight ahead with a telltale "but" to make his confession of faith. But it is not just the poet's creed that surfaces; it is also the doctor's, the solemn declaration of someone who sees and describes the cultural conditions of an age in pathological terms. In this case, Williams chooses ankylosis, the stiffening of a joint caused by abnormal bone fusion, as his metaphor for rigid aesthetic conventions from which modernism has broken away; yet diagnosis is a beginning, not an end, and the rhetoric of Williams's declaration is also that of a pledge, an artist's version of the doctor's Hippocratic oath. An age newly "broken away from its ankylosed conditions," into freedom and suppleness, will need support and supervision during its recovery; it will need not just poetic but several measures to organize its "assemblies," meaning perhaps both the assemblings of men and women in groups and the acts assembling men and women perform, as they build new forms out of the broken pieces of the old.

Along with poet and doctor speaks a man. Obviously, this particular man is not afraid of creeds, oaths, and commitments. Instead, he seems to seek these, revealing a tendency which distinguishes him. In his critical prose this tendency often surfaces as a fervor or zeal, which attracts some as it exasperates others. Whatever the responses, though, we cannot miss·the sobering tone of the final sentence: "We cannot escape it as intelligent men." The antecedent of "it," which signifies the fate of intelligent people, or at least the

fate of this particular intelligent man, is ambiguous. Is "it" the pro-
motion of poetic measure to which Williams dedicates himself? Is it
the age and its new conditions? Is it the act of dedication itself,
because, Williams may be saying, intelligent men and women need
to dedicate themselves to something? Here is one of Weatherhead's
hit-or-miss moments. Some might argue, and with good reason, that
an ambiguous referent exemplifies the sort of imprecision which
disqualifies Williams's critical prose from serious consideration. Others might counter, with equal justice, that an occasional ambiguous
referent cannot help but appear in the prose of a busy (and, by 1959,
very sick) man who was uninterested in taking the time or making
the effort to write impeccable criticism. I would suggest a third
position: In discussing poetic measure, among other measures, Williams moves toward the idea of fate, or something we cannot escape,
and the ambiguous relation of poetic measure to fate is precisely the
point.

This study examines the ambiguous, varied, and competing
meanings of "measure" in the mind and art of William Carlos Williams. Because Williams uses the term primarily in the context of
prosody and poetic form, the first two chapters will consider the
ways in which his search for a new measure realizes itself in his
poems. Chapter 1 considers the role enjambment plays in Williams's
verse, and chapter 2 discusses visual techniques and typographic
measurements. Recent scholarship indicates a growing understanding of Williams's verse schemes, an understanding that frees us from
the error of discussing his prosodic measure in the pseudo-quantitative terms of time units and pauses.[7] Despite his observation that
"Williams himself had an eye for the appearance of the printed
poem,"[8] Weatherhead makes this mistake, and others still labor under it; yet essays by Eleanor Berry and Marjorie Perloff and a full-
length study by Henry Sayre collectively advance the discussion of
Williams's measure in important ways.[9] Berry concentrates on Williams's development of a "sight-stanza," a visual grid he lays across
a text, cutting "the flow of language into visually equal segments,"
thus "defamiliarizing individual words and the manner of their syn-
tactical relations" (p. 26); Perloff shows how Williams shifted "to a
syntax that purposely goes *against* the line, blocking its integrity,"
while she also argues, in respect to *Paterson*, that "the *page* rather

than the foot or line or stanza becomes the unit of measure" (pp. 166, 183); and Sayre suggests that "At the most fundamental level, the experience of Williams' 'visual text' is roughly analogous to the experience of a concrete poem" (p. 6). I do not think the timing of these studies a simple coincidence. Instead, I sense that, a full generation after Williams's death, we are now able to reexamine and reevaluate not only his own dicta, but also the earlier formulations of those who were perhaps too close to the poet and his time.

In my discussion of enjambment and typography, I continue the inquiry Berry, Perloff, and Sayre have begun, bringing to it literary historical, diachronic considerations I find missing from their respective arguments.[10] Specifically, Wordsworth, Keats, Emerson, Whitman, Poe, Pound, and Eliot figure in my argument, as they could not be expected to in the limited spaces of Berry's or Perloff's essays or in Sayre's study of Williams's relation to the visual arts. Furthermore, none of these three considers the larger, figurative meanings of measure, as I do in chapter 3, which explores the relation of poetic to other measures, as well as the relation of poetic measure to limitations we cannot—or do not want to—escape. Remembering himself as a young medical student trying to determine what place poetry should have in his life, Williams proclaims in his *Autobiography*, "My furious wish was to be normal, undrunk, balanced in everything."[11] A furious wish for normalcy, sobriety, and balance would seem unlikely to be fulfilled, because, usually, we do not associate fury with the qualities Williams wants to possess; yet the paradox implicit in his statement informs his search for measure. I hope to show that measure provided Williams with a poetic ideology and an existential mythology which originated in this furious wish.


Behind the ambiguous, varied, and competing meanings of measure stands Whitman. In Williams's thinking Whitman embodied poetic freedom collapsed into formlessness. In a recent study, Stephen Tapscott argues that "For Williams and Pound and other poets, Whitman provides an available image of a formal predecessor."[12] But for Williams, Whitman's image, at once encouraging and daunting, initiates a "deceptively simple dance of avoidance and appropriation," as "Williams summons Whitman both as a predecessor and as a failed model, whose 'failure' to complete his experiments requires Williams' modern completions."[13] Tapscott's account of Williams's attitude toward Whitman is sound and convincing, although his remarks on prosody are not.[14] Williams's theory of measure assumes that Whitman began work which twentieth-century poets must continue.

By 1917, in "America, Whitman, and the Art of Poetry," Williams had already coined a phrase he invoked for the rest of his life: " 'free verse' is a misnomer"; all verse "must be governed."[15] That Eliot makes a similar claim in his essay "Reflections on *Vers Libre*," published eight months before, would appear to be more than a coincidence.[16] But whereas Eliot contends in that essay that the most interesting verse either takes a simple form and constantly withdraws from it or takes no form and constantly approximates a simple one, Williams does not define a governing principle for verse. The word "measure" does not appear in the essay, nor does traditional prosody command much respect: "Rhythmus—and all such bunk—be damned eternally."[17] Finally, there is no explicit identification of Whitman as someone who has failed to govern his verse.

By 1932 all this had changed. In a long letter to Kay Boyle, Williams takes prosody as his subject and Whitman as his target:

> Free verse—if it ever existed—is out. Whitman was a magnificent failure. He himself in his later stages showed all the terrifying defects of his own method. Whitman to me is one broom stroke and that is all. He could not go on. . . . Whitman grew into senseless padding, bombast, bathos. His invention ended where it began. He is almost a satirist of his era, when his line itself is taken as the criterion. He evaporates under scrutiny—crumbling not into sand, surely, but into a moraine, sizable and impressive because of that.[18]

Prosody—the organization of words into lines and lines into poems—is now the standard by which Whitman must be judged. In the years between 1917 and 1932 Williams apparently decided how to approach Whitman: concentrate on his experiments with poetic form; attack his "method." In "An Approach to the Poem" (1948) he concentrates on Whitman's "formal accomplishment," stressing "the break Whitman instituted with the more established prosody and his value to us because of that."[19] In "An Essay on *Leaves of Grass*" (1955) he declares, "From the beginning Whitman realized that the matter was largely technical."[20] Here Williams works hard at recreating Whitman in his own image. Outside the verse itself, there is little or no evidence that prosody was ever Whitman's primary concern beyond the lyrical defense of organicism in the preface to the 1855 edition of *Leaves of Grass*: "The rhyme and uniformity of perfect poems show the free growth of metrical laws and bud from them as unerringly and loosely as lilacs or roses on a bush, and take shapes as compact as the shapes of chestnuts and melons and pears, and shed the perfume impalpable to form."[21]

Williams depicts Whitman as someone who could not be expected to know what he was about:

> He didn't know any better. He didn't have the training to construct his verses after a conscious mold which would have given him power over them to turn them this way, then that, at will. He only knew how to give them birth and to release them to go their own way. He was preoccupied with the great ideas of the time, to which he was devoted, but after all, poems are made out of words not ideas. He never showed any evidence of knowing this and the unresolved forms consequent upon his beginnings remained in the end just as he left them.[22]

Whitman knew very well that poems are made of words. His celebration of his native language extends throughout his work, while his "American Primer" shows that he experienced acutely the reality of individual words, their sounds, their etymologies, their mystery. In the above passage Williams seems willfully perverse with respect to his image of Whitman. The culmination of these apparently purposeful misconstruings—what influence-theorists would call "misreadings"—appears in a brief note entitled "The American Idiom" (1960):

> Whitman lived in the nineteenth century but he, it must be acknowledged, proceeded instinctively by rule of thumb and a tough head, correctly, in the construction of his verses.

He knew nothing of the importance of what he had stumbled on, unconscious of the concept of the variable foot.[23]

Williams completes the process of dismantling and rebuilding Whitman as a lesser version of himself by claiming that the variable foot, Williams's own invention, was the discovery upon which Whitman unconsciously stumbled but which he failed to recognize. The later poet, in a characteristic mode, has projected his concerns into the work of his predecessor. This late image of Whitman as a frustrated technician following his instincts has little in common with the original image of him as a passionate man who invited his readers to be themselves. This representation occasionally takes a reductive turn, as when Williams declares: "He cleaned the decks, did little else."[24] We might prefer to overlook this kind of statement as inappropriate to a thoughtful mind; yet it does reflect the psychological setting out of which comes the theory of measure. Still, if the theory may have been motivated in part by one poet's anxiety toward Whitman, it extends beyond that anxiety to the basic issues facing writers and readers of twentieth-century nonmetrical verse.

Williams's attempts to formulate a theory of measure lie scattered throughout his work. Posthumously published, his entry on "Free Verse" contributed to the *Princeton Encyclopedia of Poetry and Poetics* demonstrates one aspect of this theorizing:

> FREE VERSE. A term popularly, but not accurately, used to describe the poems of Walt Whitman and others whose verse is based not on the recurrence of stress accent in a regular, strictly measurable pattern, but rather on the irregular rhythmic cadence of the recurrence, with variations, of significant phrases, image patterns, and the like.[25]

Although the opening reference to Whitman and the qualification "popularly, but not accurately" are both original with Williams, manuscript evidence shows that the actual definition is not.[26] An unidentified person, perhaps an editor, suggested the insertion of everything after "Walt Whitman." With two or three slight changes Williams incorporated the passage verbatim. His own original formulation, described in the entry as an "addition to the definition given above," places a different emphasis:

[W]henever and however, either by the agency of the eye or
ear, a persistent irregularity of the metrical pattern is established in a poem, it can justly be called f.v. [free verse]. The
irregularity involves both the eye and the ear. Whether the
measure be written down with a view to the appearance of
the poem on the printed page or to the sound of the words
as spoken or sung is of no consequence so long as the established irregularity is maintained.

In this context "measure" seems to mean both the pattern by
which "persistent irregularity" is recognized and that irregularity
itself. The pattern may be auditory or visual as long as it provides
a standard against which to measure irregularities. Verse in which
auditory or visual patterns vary persistently may "justly" be called
free verse. The problem with this definition is that it admits into
the category of free verse borderline cases which do not belong there.
In a sense every effective prosodic pattern varies persistently. A
trochee substitutes for an iamb, a pentameter norm gives way to a
line of nine or eleven syllables, endstopped lines yield to enjambed
ones. Variation is part of all verse. Without it readers would be
hypnotized into senselessness. Poe recognizes this in his essay "The
Rationale of Verse" in which he speaks of the need to rescue a reader
from the "perception of monotone" in a poem. Adopting the terminology of Leigh Hunt's essay "The Principle of Variety in Uniformity," Poe argues with Hunt: "Of course there is no principle in
the case—nor in maintaining it. The 'Uniformity' is the principle—
the 'Variety' is but the principle's natural safeguard from self-destruction by excess of self."[27] For Poe, Uniformity establishes the
ground against which Variety emerges as figure, whereas for Williams, at least in this late essay, Variety itself seems to establish the
ground, or the measure, of free verse.

All verse must be free to the extent that it must be able to vary
itself in order to escape self-destruction. The question is what kind
of regularity varied with what kind of irregularity produces free
verse. The irregularity must be "persistent," according to Williams.
If so, how persistent? If irregularity seems to be the rule and regularity the exception, does that yield free verse? The unidentified
person may have had these same questions when he wrote to suggest

the insertion. By incorporating it, Williams limits the meanings of "measure" to include only those patterns not based on stress accent or other "strictly" measurable criteria, such as the number of syllables in a line.

What kind of measure does that leave? Recurrent cadences, phrases, image patterns, and "the like" can establish a measurable, measuring pattern; yet Williams also has other ideas. The entry closes with this paragraph:

> The crux of the question is measure. In f[ree] v[erse] the measure has been loosened to give more play to vocabulary and syntax—hence, to the mind in its excursions. The bracket of the customary foot has been expanded so that more syllables, words, or phrases can be admitted into its confines. The new unit thus created may be called the "variable foot," a term and a concept already accepted widely as a means of bringing the warring elements of freedom and discipline together. It rejects the standard of the conventionally fixed foot and suggests that measure varies with the idiom by which it is employed and the tonality of the individual poem. Thus, as in speech, the prosodic pattern is evaluated by criteria of effectiveness and expressiveness rather than mechanical syllable counts. The verse of genuine poetry can never be "free," but f[ree] v[erse], interpreted in terms of the variable foot, removes many artificial obstacles between the poet and the fulfillment of the laws of his design.

The crux of the question (What is free verse?) is measure. In free verse the measure must establish a pattern without resorting to the metrical conventions of accentual-syllabism. That pattern having been established, Variety will emerge in the form of irregularity, loosening the verse to give more play "to the mind in its excursions." This suggestive phrase stands unexpanded. As Emily Wallace argues, "Williams wanted the measured form of the poem to provide a space for the dance of his thoughts, the flight of the winged deformities, the unpredictable variables, the music of the spoken language."[28] Wallace refers to one of Williams's favorite tropes, the dance, a formal arrangement in which, Williams believed, poetry had its origin. But just as Williams's idea of a dance implies a formal arrangement that is not rigid, so his idea of a measured poem implies a design that is fulfilled not by the "customary" and "conventional," which Williams associates with words such as "bracket," "confines," "fixed," "mechanical," and "artificial," but with the action or motion of "play," which he associates with "loosened," "expanded," "admitted," "expressiveness," and "individual."

For Williams free verse implies a network of oppositions, all of which refract the central opposition between "the warring elements of freedom and discipline." In the final paragraph of one of his last theoretical statements Williams takes the opportunity to advertise his variable foot a bit falsely, implying that the variable foot lies behind all free verse, not just a handful of poems written by William Carlos Williams in the fifties; yet from the variable foot he draws a large moral: nonmetrical verse, inaccurately called "free," is the form of freedom and discipline at war. To Williams prosodic structure represents a conflict of opposites that returns us to his ambivalence toward Whitman. He gave poets freedom; let them seek discipline so as not to abuse that freedom. At this point Williams is a long way from his stance of 1917 in "America, Whitman, and the Art of Poetry":

> Imagine too much liberty! Where is there more liberty that I may go and get a bucketful of it? If they mean that in running loose one runs amuck—why what will I care for fools. But if by "too much freedom" they mean that a man binds himself by ignoring the truths that he cannot escape, no matter how hard he may run, then I will listen.[29]

The final paragraph of "Free Verse" is the statement of a man who has come to believe in the need for discipline and a prosody based on that need. During the fifty years preceding "Free Verse," Williams's search for measure represents the search for a way to accommodate these unavoidable conclusions.

In "Free Verse" Williams admits that his measure can be auditory *or* visual, but in "Studiously Unprepared," a notebook containing entries from May 1940 to April 1941, he insists that what he seeks lies in the sound of verse:

> What I must have is a new MEASURE which I have already achieved instinctively but which I have not yet found. It will

not be a *visual* division of the parts of a poem into units but must have its basis in a fuller conception of the poetic foot—in the SOUND, that is, of the poem.[30]

When pressed by an undergraduate at one of his readings, he is forced to concede the importance of visual criteria. The student asks, "Is the division [of lines and stanzas] visual?" Williams answers:

No. Not entirely—but perhaps so, actually, I had to acknowledge. For lack of better means. An attempt to arrange the material of the verse NOT by common stress or ordinary quantity but an attempt to arrange it after a metrical pattern that ignores other basis [sic] than trial BY EAR & failing that—convenience.[31]

The picture of Williams struggling to define what he already has achieved "instinctively" recalls his own sketch of Whitman proceeding "instinctively by rule of thumb and a tough head."

Four years later he considers the same problem of line division in his unpublished "Dartmouth College Talk" (1945):

Why have I divided my lines as I have. I don't know. If I did I'd know the answer to form. I have refused to divide them according to a form I know is NOT the answer. I have attempted to discover, to tentatively feel. Somehow or other the old line must be br[o]ken up—somehow. Pleasure, pleasure to the era [ear?] is a solid guide. Knowing that we must arrive at formal limits, strict if ample in the end.[32]

Knowing "the answer to form" assumes there is a question of form. Williams does not say what that question is, but we might guess from the context. If he is thinking generally about the warring elements of freedom and discipline, the question of form might be: How do poets use their freedom from old formal limits to arrive at new ones? If he is thinking more specifically about the prosody of the nonmetrical line, as the passage indicates, the question of form might be: How can lineation alone do the work of measuring verse? His many theoretical statements suggest that he never fully believed that it could; yet his poems demonstrate that his prosody of lineation, based on techniques of enjambment and typographic patterning, led him to "formal limits, strict if ample in the end," limits that suggested to Williams the larger truths he could not escape.

# CHAPTER ONE

# Why Have I Divided My Lines
# as I Have

The red paper box
hinged with cloth

is lined
inside and out
with imitation
leather

—"Composition"

Through its root, "enjambment" inherits the meaning "to straddle"
(*enjamber*). To straddle is to sit or stand astride something with one
leg (*jamb*) on either side of it. In any enjambment syntax divides
into two legs which straddle the line terminus. Searching for the
variable foot, Williams discovered instead the straddled leg. First
published as the twelfth poem in *Spring and All* (1923) and later titled
"Composition" in *Collected Earlier Poems*, the following demonstrates
the straddling of lines by syntax:

The red paper box
hinged with cloth

is lined
inside and out
with imitation
leather

It is the sun
the table

with dinner
on it for
these are the same—

Its twoinch trays
have engineers
that convey glue
to airplanes

or for old ladies
that darn socks
paper clips
and red elastics—

What is the end
to insects
that sucked gummed
labels?

for this is eternity
through its
dial we discover
transparent tissue
on a spool

But the stars
are round
cardboard
with a tin edge

and a ring
to fasten them
to a trunk
for the vacation—[1]

In the prose preceding the poem, Williams asserts, "It is a step over from the profitless engagements of the arithmetical." The verse composition of this poem shows no engagements of the arithmetical; there is nothing to count, or at least nothing arithmetical to count on. Stanzas have from two to five lines. Lines have from two to seven syllables, a limit that keeps stresses down to no more than two per line, although to note this may be merely to "assert a trivial correlation built into the structure of English," not to identify the principle of verse composition.[2] As for auditory patterns, occasional assonance ("table," "same," "trays," "convey," "airplanes," "vacation") and alliteration ("dial we discover / transparent tissue") emerge, but these features are not prominent enough to establish a governing principle. Instead, the dominant feature of the verse scheme is the straddling of lines by sentences:

> is lined
> inside and out
> with imitation
> leather

> But the stars
> are round
> cardboard

In the first example, the line ending "imitation" produces the fleeting impression that "imitation" is a noun, an impression strengthened by Williams's statements about "W. S." (William Shakespeare) and imitation a page earlier: "his buoyancy of imagination raised him NOT TO COPY them [his fellows], not to holding the mirror up to them but to equal, to surpass them as a creator of knowledge, as a vigorous, living force above their heads" (*I*, p. 122). But in Williams's composition of physical objects, this impression is subverted when we pass to "leather" and discover the essential cheapness of the box, a cheapness Williams elevates and dignifies with his description of it as "the sun" and "eternity." In the second example, the image of the stars is also deflated, as we cross from "round" to "cardboard"; yet by the end of "Composition" we have been forced to pay attention to cardboard stars, to discover the "transparent tissue" of imitation which connects them to the eternity of real ones. The straddling of lines by sentences dramatizes "the larger processes of the imagination" (*I*, p. 123) as the poem disguises and reveals connections between words and objects.

But the word "enjambment" appears nowhere in Williams's published writing. If he had not encountered the term earlier in his reading, he would have found it in Saintsbury's *Manual of English*

*Prosody*, which he studied in 1945.[3] At any rate the omission is
striking for two reasons. First, one would think that Williams's many
attempts at critical self-definition would lead sooner or later to a few
remarks on a technique he uses so frequently. Second, beyond Williams's own poetry lies the work of his contemporaries in which
enjambment is also prevalent. Marianne Moore and E. E. Cummings
both use enjambment in bold ways, and Williams's letters and essays
show him to be a close reader of each. When discussing the problem
of line division in "Studiously Unprepared" or "Dartmouth College
Talk," Williams could have taken the opportunity to examine the
nature and importance of enjambment in modern poetry; yet only
once does he come close to acknowledging enjambment as a formal
device with traditions and conventions of its own. In the posthumously published essay "Free Verse," Williams blames Milton for
deforming the natural speech patterns of English, but then interrupts
the attack to give him some credit: "This deformity is most marked
in Milton—despite the fact that Milton in some ways anticipated
the effects of f[ree] v[erse]—and his techniques, minus his talent,
helped to create the artificial diction typical of much 18th- and 19th-
c. poetry."[4] Milton's blank verse anticipates the "effects" of free verse
by abandoning rhyme and using the line ending to wreak havoc on
the sentence. Along with Miltonic enjambments come caesurae, as
lines end in midsentence and sentences in midline. Although these
devices form only part of the Miltonic legacy to modern verse, they
form the one part Williams chooses to affirm.

John Hollander discusses the Miltonic legacy in his essay " 'Sense
Variously Drawn Out': On English Enjambment," in which he draws
this comparison between Milton and Williams:

> When enjambment is systematic, as in *Paradise Lost* or some
> of William Carlos Williams's free verse, a wide range of effects
> ensures that even strong, pointed cuts at line breaks will never
> startle by their mere occurrence but, if at all, for what they
> reveal—about language, about the world, or because of when
> and where, in the course of the poem, they show it.[5]

When enjambment is "systematic," it can become the rule rather
than the exception in a given instance. There is, however, a crucial
difference between the roles enjambment plays in *Paradise Lost* and

in the poetry of William Carlos Williams. Miltonic enjambment works within the boundaries of blank verse. Its systematic operation combines with that of an iambic pentameter norm. Without that metrical norm the systematic operation of enjambment can become the main principle of prosodic organization. This is the case with much of Williams's verse. Enjambment determines lineation, and lineation determines nonmetrical verse. Dr. Johnson's criticism of Milton's blank verse becomes even more appropriate for much of Williams's free verse:

> The variety of pauses, so much boasted by the lovers of blank verse, changes the measures of an English poet to the periods of a declaimer; and there are only a few skilful and happy readers of Milton, who enable their audience to perceive where the lines end or begin. *Blank Verse*, said an ingenious critick, *seems to be verse only to the eye.*[6]

As Hollander suggests, Dr. Johnson's comment seems "hard-of-hearing"; Milton's iambic pentameter rings in the ear long after the eye turns away. In the case of "Composition," however, Dr. Johnson would have a stronger case. To the extent that enjambment is primarily visual rather than auditory, Dr. Johnson would be right. This is verse to the eye.

But Williams developed the role of enjambment beyond its Miltonic limits. The history of this development begins with his early imitation of Keats. Modeled on *Endymion*, Williams's verse romance "Philip and Oradie" has been dated as early as 1905–06 and as late as 1908–09. The account he gives of the poem in his *Autobiography* ends with its destruction: "Then, in disgust, one day, perhaps through my impatience with my 'heroics,' I took the voluminous script, and running downstairs before I should begin to 'think,' opened the furnace door and in with it!"[7] Perhaps two copies of the manuscript originally existed, one of which Williams burned, having sent the other to Viola Baxter, later Mrs. Virgil Jordan. Perhaps the burning of the manuscript became a convenient fiction behind which to hide an early failure. Whatever the truth, the unfinished poem survives in handwritten copy:

> When chivalry like summer's crimson fruit
> From blossom, April's flimsy pride and all

The ripening seasons, burst at length full frocked
Resplendant [sic] on her prime; when kings were young
And liegemen bold ambitious and full oft
Of equal blood with sovrans lived a knight
Don Pedro was he clept, Prince of Navarre;
An Agramant [?], who loved in eager toil,
Defiant, still to bruise those heraldries,
Though forty years of heyday wasting war
Had grated up his front. Oh I could sing
Of his brave deeds until the harking throng
Cloyed with flat peace would fly like midnight birds
Into the sudden flame and hell of passion
Heedless of torment toppling kingdoms down—
But to what end?[8]

In this "Introduction" to "Philip and Oradie" enjambment operates within the iambic pentameter norm of blank verse. The lack of consistent punctuation makes it difficult to tell partially stopped lines from unstopped ones, but the most striking instances of enjambment stand out clearly: "crimson fruit / From blossom"; "all / the ripening seasons"; "full oft / Of equal blood"; "I could sing / Of his brave deeds"; "like midnight birds / Into the sudden flame." Although Williams acknowledges the influence of *Endymion* (*Endymion* is written in couplets), the deeper prosodic influence comes from his model's model, *Paradise Lost*. By 1909, when Williams published *Poems*, he had discovered the Miltonic technique of drawing out sense from one line to another. At the end of the second line above, for example, "all" hangs between adjectival and pronominal status. Williams's enjambment places the adjective "all" in final stressed position, underscoring the totality of the seasonal cycle, the mythical copresence of fruit and blossom. In the romance world of "Philip and Oradie" all the ripening seasons cooperate in a simile for youth and vigor, bursting forth on cue, unlike the spring Williams would describe as "Lifeless in appearance, sluggish / dazed" fifteen years later in a book about spring—and all.

By Williams's own account *The Wanderer*, first published in 1914, took the place of "Philip and Oradie" after its "destruction."[9] In this poem the restrictions of blank verse have been eased, but traces of its long pentameter line remain:

> I saw her eyes straining at the new distance
> And as the woods fell from her flying
> Likewise they fell from me as I followed
> So that I strongly guessed all that I must put from me
> To come through ready for the high courses.
>
> But one day, crossing the ferry
> With the great towers of Manhattan before me,
> Out at the prow with the sea wind blowing,
> I had been wearying many questions
> Which she had put on to try me:
> How shall I be a mirror to this modernity?[10]

For the most part in this passage Williams avoids oddities of syntax and diction, with the possible exceptions of "strongly guessed" and "wearying many questions." As in "Philip and Oradie," the absence of consistent punctuation makes it difficult to judge when a line could be considered partially stopped; yet even with this lack of punctuation, the passage contains no striking examples of enjambment. Are these lines barely enjambed or barely endstopped? Each of the first four lines, as well as the ninth and tenth, contains a single clause, either independent or subordinate. Against the background of this pattern the transition from the fourth line to the fifth becomes the most daring, as it continues a clause beyond a line boundary. Also striking is the absence of caesurae in these lines. In giving up the patterns of Miltonic blank verse, Williams temporarily sacrifices the effects that result from setting the line against the sentence. In this passage from *The Wanderer* he prefers long, unbroken lines that sweep from left to right. The steady, smooth succession of such lines suits the meditative mood of "Advent" in which the Wanderer contemplates the nature of his poetic project.

In the later books of *Collected Earlier Poems* the systematic operations of enjambment reappear with little trace of their Miltonic origin. With a few exceptions, such as "The Yachts," the poems use shorter lines than those of "Philip and Oradie" or *The Wanderer*. In a poem where enjambments occur at the ends of ten- or twelve-syllable lines, those enjambments work locally, strongly affecting the beginnings and endings of lines, while exerting little immediate pressure on the middles. In a systematically enjambed short-line poem this changes. Suddenly, there is little left in a line that can be called its "middle." Instead, it has a head which inherits a syntactic remainder from the previous line and a tail where the next enjambment waits. The short-line poem is in a state of constant enjambment. In nonmetrical verse short-line enjambments determine lineation directly, unlike their metrical, long-line counterparts. They have the immediate power to influence the grouping of successive words into successive lines. This grouping of successive elements (words) and events (lineations) becomes the basis of prosody in nonmetrical verse. This prosody is neither temporal nor accentual. For lack of a more precise terminology I will call it "phenomenological." Enjambing lineation cuts a word off from its immediate context and holds it up for inspection, highlighting it among its neighbors. One might want to describe this highlighting in temporal or accentual terms, saying enjambment causes the reader to "pause," "hesitate," or "emphasize," but these terms, borrowed from quantitative or accentual metrical systems, remain figurative with respect to nonmetrical verse.

First published in *Smoke* (Autumn 1934) and later included in *An Early Martyr* (1935), this poem is a study in nonmetrical short-line enjambment:


To a Poor Old Woman

munching a plum on
the street a paper bag
of them in her hand

They taste good to her
They taste good
to her. They taste
good to her

> You can see it by
> the way she gives herself
> to the one half
> sucked out in her hand
>
> Comforted
> a solace of ripe plums
> seeming to fill the air
> They taste good to her                    [*CEP*, p. 99]

If the title also serves as the first line, four quatrains contain lines of three to six syllables. Neither accents, nor syllables, nor sounds establish any dominant pattern in the poem. Aside from the lineation itself, the most obvious structural feature is the repetition of the sentence "They taste good to her." Twice the sentence occupies a single line, and twice it is broken around line endings. Enjambments redistribute its words, placing now one, now another at the head or tail of a line. Without an accentual-syllabic norm, it is impossible to convert any of these redistributions into stress values. Does the first line of the second stanza ("They taste good to her") mean they taste good as opposed to *bad*? If so, we might say the second sentence ("They taste good / to her") means they taste good *to her*, because she is easily pleased, but to someone more discriminating they might taste bad. We are left with the third sentence ("They taste / good to her"), which could mean that although the plums look and smell awful, they *taste* great. In each case enjambment leads the reader to interpret lineation as a guide to meaning, but it does not dictate that meaning. We can imagine further redistributions which Williams does not give:

> They taste good to
> her.
>
> They
> taste good to her.

Here redistribution is even more radical, as it sets off single words, placing them in their own lines. In the one-word line enjambment and lineation merge. The question of stress value becomes extraneous. In the first case, separation of "her" from "to" would continue a pattern Williams establishes with the enjambments "on / the street" and "by / the way." As the object "her" detached itself from its preposition, the isolation of the old woman would be confirmed. In the second case, the plums would receive more attention, suggesting that plums and only plums taste good to the old woman.

An old woman stands on the street munching ripe plums. Enjoying their good taste may be the best thing that happens to her all day. The phrase "the way she gives herself" hints that the poet recognizes an erotic force in the pleasure that the plums give the old woman. Williams builds "To a Poor Old Woman" around this simple, homely image. How does enjambment enhance meaning? The sentence "They taste good to her" rests in the first line of the second stanza wholly intact. Line and sentence stand integrated. With the second, third, and fourth lines fragmentation occurs. Lines contain bits and pieces of sentences; sentences twist and turn across lines. It is not until the final line of the poem that Williams picks up the pieces and restores them to wholeness: "They taste good to her." Enjambment works with lineation to establish a circular pattern, as the poem moves from wholeness through fragmentation and back to wholeness. This pattern exists apart from the image of the old woman. She has been quietly munching her plums the entire time.

The circular passage from wholeness through fragmentation and back takes place in the mind of the poet observing the woman. It is as though he has been savoring the possibilities of English syntax as she savors the plums. Enjambment dramatizes the transformation of the poet's initial observation ("They taste good to her") into verse: How shall I lineate this observation? Which of its elements do I want to frame? He divides it first one way, then another, sacrificing its original integrity to the fragmentation of analysis. The poet's consciousness turns to the versifier's self-consciousness. Through his identification with her, however, wholeness is restored to his original observation. The one-word line "Comforted" invites special attention, because it is the only such line in the poem. Who is comforted? Capitalization would suggest that the fourth stanza begins a new sentence, but the old woman is nowhere to be found in that stanza, having been mentioned last in the third. Certainly she is comforted, but so is the poet. The plums taste good to her. When he apprehends that in its totality, her solace becomes his.

From *Collected Earlier Poems* on, the boundaries of lines do not coincide with the boundaries of sentences. Charles Hartman calls this disjunction "counterpoint," including under that heading any "significant conflict" between nonmetrical modes of organization.[11] Presumably these modes could take many forms, both visual and auditory. For Williams, however, the primary form of counterpointing arises with line-sentence disjunctions, which produce enjambments and caesurae. In *Collected Earlier Poems* these disjunctions extend into the realm of word-splitting, a type of enjambment that occurs rarely in Williams's early poetry.[12] Between 1944 and 1950 it appears frequently. Some of Williams's formations include: "resent- / ment"; "grad- / ually"; "o- / dors"; "dis- / tinction"; "affec- / tionate"; and "conceptu- / ally."[13] In "The Banner Bearer," first published in 1946, word-splitting establishes the dominant prosodic pattern:

> In the rain, the lonesome
> dog idiosyn-
> cratically, with each
> quadribeat, throws
>
> out the left fore-
> foot beyond
> the right intent, in
> his stride,
>
> on some obscure
> insistence—from bridge-
> ward going
> into new terrority.                    [*CLP*, p. 81]

The three word-splitting enjambments mime the slight hitch in a dog's gait. As he trots alone through the rain, he kicks out one front paw slightly more than the other. The dog becomes an image of rhythmic timekeeping. When his left forepaw kicks out on the "quadribeat," a new four-beat measure begins. By means of these enjambments, more daring than the others in the poem, Williams creates the illusion of quantitative temporality in his poem, punc-

tuating it with the signs of periodicity. The first enjambment ("idio-
syn- / cratically") comes before we know what it means. Perhaps
Williams is using enjambment idiosyncratically to set off a long word
among short ones. With the second enjambment ("fore- / foot") the
identification becomes explicit. It establishes a pattern. The third
enjambment ("bridge- / ward") projects the dog's rhythmic grid out
from the dog onto an expanding landscape that opens before him
and us. His stride measures out new territory with "some obscure /
insistence." A lonely dog in the rain beating out time idiosyncratically—Williams sees in this figure something of himself bearing the
banner of free verse into undiscovered regions.

Beyond the local meanings in a particular poem lies the general
significance of word-splitting enjambment. Whereas we usually think
of a single word as the basic unit of both the sentence and the line,
the division of this unit into smaller units dramatizes the building
of words out of subverbal blocks of meaning. Splitting a word across
a line boundary momentarily magnifies the discrete parts of which
the whole is composed. The moving picture of language slows down,
and we apprehend fully one of the thousands of subliminal images
being flashed all the time. The impression is necessarily brief, as we
would soon cease to be effective users of language if we were forever
pausing to marvel at the sudden strangeness of words dissolved into
fractions of words. Compared to Cummings's extensive use of this
technique, Williams's word-splittings are tame:

> the(oo)is
>
> lOOk
> (aliv
> e)e
> yes
>
> are(chIld)and
>
> wh(g
> o
> ne)
> o
>
> w(A)a(M)s[14]

Here Cummings enjambs the words "alive," "eyes," "who," and "gone." With the line "e)e" he produces an image of eyes, separated by a nose. With the enjambment "e / yes," an affirmative "yes" detaches itself from "eyes" and the vision they afford. The word "who" contains a parenthetical "gone," "gone" yields "go" and "one," and the "o's" of "who" and "gone" line up to echo the two sets of eyelike double "o's" in the first two lines. Encoded in the poem is a statement about the perceiving self (the upper-case "I" in "chIld" puns on "eye"), the visual, and perhaps visionary, acts of looking and seeing, and the passage of time. The child who was and is now gone surfaces in the last line to declare "I AM." Williams never produced poems like this one. His comment on Cummings's poem "(im)c-a-t(mo)," quoted in Book Five of *Paterson*, suggests how he would have reacted to poems such as "the(oo)is": "I would reject it as a poem. . . . I get no meaning at all."[15]

Unlike Marianne Moore, Williams could not justify splitting words to meet the demands of syllabic verse:

> All
> external
> > marks of abuse are present on this
> > defiant edifice—
> > > all the physical features of
>
> ac-
> cident—lack
> > of cornice, dynamite grooves, burns, and
> > hatchet strokes, these things stand
> > > out on it; the chasm-side is
>
> dead.                                                    ["The Fish"][16]

Here Moore is working with a 1-3-9-6-8 syllabic scheme, as well as with a rhyme scheme of *aabbx*. The enjambment "ac- / cident" not only fulfills the design of Moore's prosodic scheme, but it also splits one of her many Latinate words into its etymological components (*ad*, "to" and *cadere*, "to fall"). The physical features of a cliff record what has fallen upon or happened to it, accidental operations of human and natural forces. Despite his admiration of Moore ("Marianne Moore is of all American writers most constantly a poet" [*I*, p. 145]), Williams did not use her syllabic techniques. The word-splitting technique recedes in *The Desert Music* and *Journey to Love* and occurs seldom in *Pictures from Brueghel*.

Having defined the extreme for himself, Williams returns in his last three books to the types of enjambment found in *Collected Earlier Poems*. In his triadic stanza poems of the fifties, line-sentence counterpointings cooperate with an indentation pattern to produce new effects; because the change is mainly typographic, the triadic stanza will be discussed in the next chapter. In the ten-poem sequence "Pictures from Brueghel," first published in 1960, line-sentence counterpointing takes an interesting turn. Williams does not employ any radically new types of enjambment, but he uses the technique in a different setting, as in the third poem, "The Hunters in the Snow":

> The over-all picture is winter
> icy mountains
> in the background the return
>
> from the hunt it is toward evening
> from the left
> sturdy hunters lead in
>
> their pack the inn-sign
> hanging from a
> broken hinge is a stag a crucifix
>
> between his antlers the cold
> inn yard is
> deserted but for a huge bonfire
>
> that flares wind-driven tended by
> women who cluster
> about it to the right beyond
>
> the hill is a pattern of skaters
> Brueghel the painter
> concerned with it all has chosen

a winter-struck bush for his
foreground to
complete the picture        .      .[17]

In order to discuss line-sentence counterpointing, one must be able to distinguish a line from a sentence. Whereas we can tell a line at a glance, it is not so simple with a sentence. A sentence must fulfill certain grammatical criteria to be a sentence; yet in reading we usually rely on the conventions of capitalization and punctuation to define its boundaries. Where one of these conventions is inconsistently maintained, as is the case with punctuation in "Philip and Oradie" or *The Wanderer*, line-sentence counterpointing can become difficult to recognize. The borders of enjambment blur. In "The Hunters in the Snow" Williams builds his poem around this ambiguity. Organized in tercets with short middle lines, the poem appears to be a model of conventional patterning and predictability. When Williams dispenses with punctuation and capitalization, however, conventional patterning and predictability go with them. Where does a sentence begin or end? Is the first line a complete sentence? If so, what is its relation to the two successive phrases "icy mountains / in the background" and "the return // from the hunt"? If not, is the first line enjambed? Take the fourth line: "from the hunt it is toward evening." The second part of it turns out to be a complete sentence, but because the line is not stopped, we read right through it, expecting something like "it is toward evening / when the moon is rising." Without punctuation we proceed from one line to the next, experiencing the form of enjambment but not the substance. We associate enjambment with running-on, but running-on is all we do in "The Hunters in the Snow." Perhaps the most complicated example comes in the final line of the fifth stanza: "about it to the right beyond." Coming into this line from the preceding one ("women who cluster"), we appropriate all of it to complete the relative clause. Suddenly, in the first line of the sixth stanza we discover "beyond" is a preposition, not an adverb, putting us in the midst of a new sentence. Where does this new sentence begin? After "about it" or "to the right"? The absence of punctuation causes us to read through a caesural stop and to stop in the middle of the genuine enjambment "beyond / the hill."

With full capitalization and punctuation "The Hunters in the Snow" would show the by now familiar operations of line-sentence counterpointing. Without these customary signposts the poem produces yet another layer of counterpointing, as significant conflict develops between the system that produces enjambments and caesurae (line-sentence counterpointing) and the system that inhibits the apprehension of these (suppression of punctuation and capitalization). The double counterpointing suits a poem about a painting, or rather, a poem about the process of looking at a painting. In "The Hunters in the Snow" poetry, a temporal medium, encounters painting, a spatial medium. The operations of enjambing lineation dramatize the sequential, successional order of verse, while the withdrawal of capitalization and punctuation threatens to subvert that order by confusing the line-sentence relationship. As we view Brueghel's picture over Williams's shoulder, we distinguish details in temporal succession, differentiating them one by one from the totality of the painting; yet there is no reason why the same details could not be apprehended in a completely different order. Mountains, hunters, inn-sign, bonfire, women, skaters, bush—the sequence represents the poem's temporal ordering of the painting's spatial elements. Double counterpointing becomes the sign of revolt against this order, as it extends the Miltonic legacy of "sense variously drawn out."

In "The Hunters in the Snow" Williams complicates the operations of enjambment so that sense is drawn out to make several readings possible. The technique is effective, as it forces a reader to work at extracting meaning from the poem as the viewer must work at distinguishing detail in Brueghel's painting. Just as Brueghel generates an illusion of simultaneous events and facts, none of which is subordinated to the hunters' return, each demanding instead its own share of attention, so Williams generates a similar illusion by refusing to subordinate syntax to the visual codes of capitalization and punctuation. When these codes disappear, the syntactic groups they regulate suddenly break in on our attention with new significance. For Williams, the winter-struck bush, which Brueghel places in his "foreground to / complete the picture" and which Williams uses to complete his poem, is an image of this new significance. An otherwise insignificant detail, the bush gets overlooked at first because it stands closest to the viewer. But after we have gone more deeply into the painting, encountering with Williams its other images and details, we return to the bush with an understanding of its place in a larger configuration. This understanding completes our experience of the picture. Williams's trope for this completion is the closure of his own poem, a poem about, among other things, how to read a painting or a poem in order to discover the relation of its parts to one another.

Enjambment is difficult to define. It takes many forms, some of which defy simple classification. *The Oxford English Dictionary (OED)* dates the first recorded usage of "enjambment" in 1837–39. In his *Historical Manual of English Prosody* (1910), Saintsbury defines enjambment as "An Englishing, on simple analogy, of the French technical term, *enjambement*, for the overlapping in sense and utterance, of one verse on another, or of one couplet on another."[18] Seventy years later in a full-length study of enjambment, Harai Golomb surveys previous definitions and proposes his own: "Enjambment is the occurrence of a line boundary at a point where the structure of the preversified text, for reasons of syntax, lingual meaning and/or literary interpretation, does not permit the oral execution or the aural imagination of a pausal juncture."[19] These two definitions represent extremes. Saintsbury, writing on the eve of modernism, cannot foresee the expanded role of enjambment in twentieth-century American free verse. According to him, enjambment occurs between metrical lines or couplets (the *OED* also defines it as "continuation of a sentence beyond the second line of a couplet"), and the vague term "overlapping" describes its operation. Golomb, writing after the recent explosion of linguistic theory, attempts a more sophisticated account, but relies on the questionable wording "does not permit" and "pausal juncture." Although he denies it, Golomb's definition veers dangerously close to the performative fallacy. He also invites time and timing into his formulation with the phrase "pausal juncture." We might wonder, for instance, how to distinguish different kinds of pausal junctures from one another. By their length? By contrast, Hollander's description of enjambment as the nonalignment of syntax and lineation avoids the traps of the overly vague, as well as the hazards of theoretical reduction.[20]

Any classification of the various types of enjambment inevitably runs into trouble. If we opt for a syntactic account rather than a "pausal" one, we must become expert linguists and grammarians prepared to define and inventory types of sentences, clauses, phrases, and other syntactic or grammatical "units." Even with its inherent ambiguity (what is a grammatical unit?), Roger Fowler's formulation summarizes the point of any such classification: "It seems that the smaller the grammatical unit concerned, the greater is its resistance to being stretched over a metrical boundary."[21] Following Fowler, Samuel Levin sketches this hierarchy of enjambments arranged in order of decreasing "resistance": enjambments between "(a) two morphemes (of a word), (b) two words (of a phrase), (c) two phrases (of a clause), (d) two clauses (of a sentence)."[22] Even with its imperfect terminology, this taxonomy suggests that if enjambments cannot be defined and classified satisfactorily in absolute terms, they can at least be described in relative ones.

This is Hollander's approach. He proposes a spectrum along which enjambments would fall according to the relative "hardness" or "softness" of the cuts they make.[23] He then cites the final line of *Paradise Lost* as an example of "total closure." Any opening up of a line to enjambment can be measured relatively against this standard. For the purpose of analysis, we shall modify Hollander's example somewhat. Our standard of total closure will be a line of poetry that contains a single sentence beginning at the left margin and extending unbroken to the right, where it ends. This one-sentence, noncaesural line owes nothing to the techniques of "sense variously drawn out"; it is a figure of self-contained wholeness:

> I pass solitary in my car.                    [*CEP*, p. 136]
>
> Must you have a part in everything?           [*CEP*, p. 153]
>
> Your petals would be quite curled up.         [*CEP*, p. 154]
>
> I am late at my singing.                      [*CEP*, p. 187]
>
> Gentlefooted crowds are treading out your lullaby.
>                                               [*CEP*, p. 192]
>
> Porters in red hats run on narrow platforms.  [*CEP*, p. 194]
>
> Love has not even visited this country.       [*CEP*, p. 207]

What the hell do you know about it?                [*CEP*, p. 282]

I make really very little money.                [*CEP*, p. 311]

This is what was intended from the first.        [*CEP*, p. 317]


These examples from Williams show the one-sentence, noncaesural line sweeping uninterrupted from left to right. All but two of them begin or end a stanza or poem. The other two constitute their own one-line stanzas in the middles of poems. In a poem composed entirely of one-sentence, noncaesural lines, enjambment would never occur, and linear wholeness would never be lost or regained. Instead, as the eye moved down the page from old line ending to new line beginning, it would experience the rhythms of constant renewal: initiation, completion, initiation, completion. Like a typewriter carriage returned, the eye would begin each successive line with a clean slate, encountering no syntactic remainder from the line above. The left margin would always be the scene of ignition, of the explosive surge forward, and the right margin the place of alighting, ending, coming in for a landing. Williams wrote no such poems. For this reason the one-sentence, noncaesural line provides a useful standard. Any deviations from the standard begin the process of measurement and interpretation. Because such deviations occur so frequently in Williams's verse, they rarely startle by their mere occurrence, but rather, as Hollander suggests, "for what they reveal—about language, about the world, or because of when or where, in the course of the poem" they make their revelations. Williams's later poem "Seafarer" demonstrates the operations of enjambment, as well as its revelations.

Williams tells in his *Autobiography* of taking a trip with Flossie to Newfoundland in 1931. He concludes the second section of the book with the statement, "It is strange to bathe alone in an Arctic sea."[24] Seventeen years later this strangeness found its way into "Seafarer." Although the Seafarer does not bathe, he is alone with an Arctic sea. First published in 1948 under the title "The Sea Farer," the poem is reprinted with a few minor revisions in *Collected Later Poems*:

> The sea will wash in
> but the rocks—jagged ribs
> riding the cloth of foam
> or a knob or pinnacles
>           with gannets—
> are the stubborn man.
>
> He invites the storm, he
> lives by it! instinct
> with fears that are not fears
> but prickles of ecstasy,
> a secret liquor, a fire
> that inflames his blood to
> coldness so that the rocks
> seem rather to leap
> at the sea than the sea
> to envelope them. They strain
> forward to grasp ships
> or even the sky itself that
> bends down to be torn
> upon them. To which he says
> It is I! I who am the rocks!
> Without me nothing laughs.                    [*CLP*, p. 170]

The poem has twenty-two lines and falls into two sections. With one exception ("with gannets—") the lines run from five to eight syllables. Although the poem shows no accentual-syllabic norm, a few lines suggest the faint trace of an iambic trimeter pattern:

> ríding the clóth of foám (initial trochaic inversion)
> with feárs that áre not feárs
> withoút me nóthing laúghs.

These scansions do not mean the lines should be read this way, because without an accentual-syllabic norm it is impossible to determine an abstract stress pattern; they simply show a recurrent tendency in the poem itself toward a regularity that could be interpreted as iambic. Even without strict accentual-syllabic design, most lines carry two or more strong stresses, perhaps because in almost any five- to eight-syllable chunk of English two or three stronger stresses will emerge. As for auditory patterns in "Seafarer," the poem shows occasional alliteration ("rocks," "ribs," "riding"), assonance ("ribs," "pinnacles," "prickles"), and consonance ("ecstasy," "rocks," "sky"), but nothing strong enough to organize the whole. Instead, line-sentence counterpointing is the dominant technique and recurrent enjambment the most striking structural feature.

When an enjambment is striking for what it reveals about the world, it is representational. Its meaning is mimetic. To produce this kind of meaning a line division must reflect thematic content. In "Seafarer" we find an interesting example:

> They strain
> forward to grasp ships
> or even the sky itself that
> bends down to be torn
> upon them.

Here are four line breaks, four enjambments. The first ("strain / forward") divides verb from adverb, two elements of what Levin would call a "phrase." The less resistant enjambment would be one between phrases, two elements of a "clause":

> They strain forward
> to grasp ships

As it stands, the verb-adverb enjambment suits the sense better. As the rocks strain forward, so the disrupted phrase strains across the line boundary. Enjambment represents that straining. There is also mimetic meaning in the placement of the word "forward" at the head of a line, the place where the forwardness of the line originates.

The second enjambment ("ships / or") divides one object of an infinitive from a conjunction joining it to the phrase containing a second object of the same infinitive. The more resistant enjambment would be one that divides two words of the same phrase, such as one splitting conjunction and conjoined:

> forward to grasp ships or
> even the sky itself that

Williams's decision to opt for a less resistant division contrasts with
the third enjambment ("that / bends"), which divides subject, a relative pronoun, from verb. The less resistant enjambment would be
one that leaves the relative clause intact:

> or even the sky itself
> that bends down to be torn

Again we can assign the more resistant enjambment a mimetic meaning: as the sky bends down to be torn upon the rocks, so the subject-
verb bond bends down around a line ending to be torn across it.
The fourth and final enjambment ("torn / upon") divides a passive
infinitive from a prepositional phrase. As a less resistant, phrasal
enjambment it completes a pattern of line division. Enjambments
between two words of the same phrase alternate with enjambments
between two phrases. This alternation between more and less resistance sets off the mimetic enjambments (in this case the more
resistant ones) from the others. The alternation between more and
less violence corresponds to the rhythms of waves crashing on rocks.
If we change the line breaks, adopting any of the alternatives above,
we change this mimetic meaning. The semantic meaning, however,
would remain unchanged.

The problem with mimetic meaning is that we can easily make
too much of it. Depending on the ingenuity of an individual reader,
every enjambment can be interpreted mimetically. In some cases
mimetic interpretation will seem strained and contrived. The reason
for this is simple: mimetic meaning does not inhere in a given enjambment; it depends on the apparent alignment of verse form and
thematic content. Where the alignment is loose, even the fastest
talking remains unconvincing. Still, if an enjambment is not strictly
mimetic, it is representational. Instead of showing something about
the world with its straining rocks or torn skies, it may show something about language, the medium itself:

> a secret liquor, a fire
> that inflames his blood to
> coldness

The enjambment "to / coldness" divides a preposition from its object. Literally, a preposition is a word "placed in front" of a substantive to indicate its relation to a verb, an adjective, or another substantive. Prepositions do the work of relating the parts of a sentence to one another. In this case, "to" relates "coldness" to the verb "inflames." How will the secret liquor, a fire, inflame his blood? To (the state of) coldness. Dividing the preposition from its object ends a line with a preposition, the sign of relation. As a single entity, then, the line "that inflames his blood to" leads out to the right margin where it leaves the reader in a state of undefined relatedness. Although this is the only example of preposition-object enjambment in "Seafarer," Williams's poetry contains many others:

| | |
|---|---|
| Let the snake wait under | [*CLP*, p. 7] |
| and foam to lay a carpet for | [*CLP*, p. 12] |
| pulled down by a weight of | [*CLP*, p. 17] |
| had cavorted down the hill in | [*CLP*, p. 36] |

Each of these lines abandons us at the moment when the fact of relatedness is established. Until we go to the next line, we cannot limit the infinite relations possible. If we think of the line as existing in a metaphorical vacuum, then once the prepositional motion towards relatedness begins, it cannot be contained: "that inflames his blood to"—anything, everything. An infinite "to-ness" continues beyond the line ending. Until we cross to the next line, the Seafarer's blood is boiling in all directions. His excitement rages uncontained, becoming part and parcel of everything. When we do cross to the next line, we discover that the object has been released from its customary role as preposition-follower and invested with the power of left-margin priority. In heading a new line, "coldness" asserts its independence from the prepositional structure. It is no longer simply the object of a preposition but a substantive momentarily abstracted from the web of conceptual relations, which syntactic arrangements signify. The enjambment of a prepositional phrase restores each element to an original separateness. Here that separateness is all the more striking, as it startles with the oxymoronic association of "inflames" and "coldness."

In addition to its representational function, whether mimetic or linguistic, enjambment carries out the work of organizing "Seafarer" prosodically into a structural whole. When or where enjambment occurs determines the basic patterns that differentiate this piece of nonmetrical verse from prose. The final line of the poem recalls our standard of measurement, the one-sentence, noncaesural line that sweeps unbroken from left to right:

>  Without me nothing laughs.

This line, as a figure of wholeness and closure, seals the poem. It is the only such line in "Seafarer." As the final line it is the culmination of structural development, the end toward which the other twenty-one lines aim. The following skeleton schematizes its structure:

>  S _____ .

The capital "S" stands for the beginning of a sentence. The period signals syntactic closure. Between the two the line rests whole. Using this skeleton, we can measure any line in the poem against it. For example:

>  S _____ /

Here the line and sentence begin together, but the sentence continues beyond the line boundary. The slant bar (/) represents enjambment. "Seafarer" contains one such line, the first:

>  The sea will wash in

The enjambment divides this clause from a second one. Departing from this first violation of line-sentence closure, "Seafarer" moves toward its final line. On the way it shows many versions of disjunction between sentence and line boundaries. Among these we can distinguish three types of structural brokenness: lines that break with an enjambment, lines that break around one or more caesurae, and lines that do both.

The caesura is to the interior of a line what enjambment is to the ending. When the line breaks, but the syntax does not, the result is enjambment. When the syntax breaks, but the line does not, the result is a caesura. Through its Latin root "caesura" means cutting off. In a line containing a caesura the sweep from left to right is momentarily cut off. Often punctuation marks the cutoff, but as seen in "The Hunters in the Snow," this is not always the case. The punctuation stop, when it appears, reflects the degree of caesural break. Periods mark a complete break, commas a less violent one. In "Seafarer" we can compare these two lines and their skeletons:

> He invites the storm, he
> S ———————, —/

> to envelope them. They strain
> ——————. S———/

Conceivably the break after "storm" could be marked by a period. As it stands, Williams's punctuation differentiates between a partial cutoff and a complete one. In the case of the partial caesura what could be divided into two complete sentences proceeds instead with the momentum of appositional variation. Although both lines end with enjambment, the momentum in the first carries force with it through the line division.

In analyzing the caesura, we must do more than distinguish between breaks of greater and lesser degree; we must also notice where in the line the caesura appears. Compare the lines above with the following:

> It is I! I who am the rocks!

In this line Williams uses the same punctuation stop to mark caesurae of different force. The first syntactic break is partial and could be marked by a comma; the second is complete and could be marked by a period. The exclamation point intensifies the partial break by signaling the abruptness of forceful utterance. In contrast to the lines above, which break around terminal caesurae, this line breaks around an initial caesura. In the short lines of "Seafarer" it is sometimes difficult to distinguish clearly initial and medial or medial and ter-

minal caesurae. Still, the combination of various types of caesural
stopping with various types of enjambment produces the most prominent features of the poem. The later in the line a caesura appears
before an enjambment, the more disruptive their combined effect
will be. On the other hand, the earlier in the line the caesura appears
after an enjambment, the more radical its intrusion will seem. Terminal caesura before enjambment fragments the last part of the line,
as the linear sweep from left to right stutters at the moment when
syntax breaks. Initial caesura after enjambment breaks up the new
line before it can establish continuity or momentum. These principles operate in the lines below:

> to envelope them. They strain
> forward to grasp ships
> or even the sky itself that
> bends down to be torn
> upon them. To which he says,
> It is I! I who am the rocks!
> Without me nothing laughs.

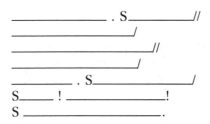

In this diagram the double slant bar (//) marks an enjambment
between two words of a phrase, whereas the single slant bar marks
any less resistant enjambment. The sequence of line skeletons begins
to look like a series of dots and dashes in Morse code. It is a type
of code, the analogue in nonmetrical verse of scansion in metrical
verse. As we read the code, we notice several important features.
In the first three sentences each successive "S," for example, appears
closer to the left, signifying a migration of syntax boundaries toward
alignment with the margins in the final line. At the same time the

disjunction between syntax and line boundaries at the right margin becomes gradually less severe until the final alignment. The final enjambment divides a relative clause (the antecedent of "which" could be the sky, the rocks, or the entire scene) from a complete sentence set in indirect discourse. This is barely enjambment at all. Notice, too, the group of three lines without caesurae. They form a kind of picture of continuity framed by discontinuity, as lines with caesurae precede and follow them. The prosody of the poem is based on these features.

In any poem sentence and line are either aligned or not aligned. In most poems sentence-line alignment mixes with nonalignment. The prosody of a poem grows out of this mixture. Is there more alignment than nonalignment? Does the poem move from alignment to nonalignment or vice versa? Does the use of enjambment and caesurae establish patterns of continuity and discontinuity? These questions can be asked of any poem, and any poem yields structural meaning in answer. "Seafarer" moves toward and closes with sentence-line alignment. Even though semantic meaning remained the same, the prosody and structural meaning would be altered if the poem ended

> It is I! I who am the rocks! Without
> me nothing
> laughs.

Instead of wholeness and alignment the poem would end in fragmentation and nonalignment. The prosodic structure of a poem tells a story about wholeness and fragmentation, a story about the world in which the poem says what it says.

The world of "Seafarer" is a world in which wholeness and alignment have the final say; yet it is also a world in which a man compares himself to jagged rocks upon which the sky bends down to be torn. The struggle between creative forces and destructive ones pervades this northern coastal seascape. In the midst of natural violence the Seafarer asserts a powerful, triumphant calm. Unlike his counterpart in the Old English elegy, Williams's Seafarer does not mourn his losses or complain of afflictions suffered on the sea; he does not seek consolation outside himself. Instead, he appropriates the rocks as self-representations. Submerged, they break the surface to threaten all that rides the sea. The surfacing of submerged presences suggests the intrusion of volatile psychic material. At the same time, however, the rocks are figures of firmness and solidity. When the Seafarer declares that he is the rocks, he invokes Biblical associations from the Old and New Testaments. God is Israel's Rock in the Pentateuch (Deuteronomy 32:4), and Peter is the rock upon which Jesus will build a church (Matthew 16:18). The Seafarer is his own rock, a rugged figure of self-reliance. He is both destroyer and sustainer. Whatever dangers an Arctic sea presents, the Seafarer defends against them by making himself the measure of all things, the rock without which nothing laughs. The structural progress from nonalignment to alignment in the poem parallels this resolution.


Discussing various styles of free verse, Paul Fussell concludes that "The principle [of excellence in each of these styles] is that every technical gesture in a poem must justify itself in meaning."[25] In the nonmetrical verse of William Carlos Williams enjambment is a common, if not the most common, "technical gesture." The gesture characterizes a prosody based not on time, accents, sounds, or recurrent phrases, but on lineation. Inevitably lineation produces arrangements that, to their credit, are perceived as "rhythmic," but in Williams's verse this rhythmic quality depends on lineation; it is not something abstract or anterior to lineation, which lineation embodies or signifies, as is the case with accentual-syllabic verse. The meanings of this gesture are many. When we interpret a given instance of enjambment mimetically, tying it to a particular feature of thematic content, we justify it locally. We say: Enjambment is appropriate here because it enacts what these words are saying. When we interpret the pattern of enjambments throughout a poem prosodically, analyzing the tendencies toward line-sentence alignment or nonalignment, we justify it generally. If we can tie this general pattern to the thematic content, so much the better; yet, like an accentual-syllabic design, the same pattern may appear in two poems which say different things, confirming that the formal pattern is also abstract and not simply an extension of content. A third level of interpretation involves a somewhat more theoretical approach in

which we attempt to justify enjambment universally or, as Justus
Lawler describes it, "transcendently." Lawler's approach assumes
that enjambment is mimetic, but that its mimetic power is not confined locally to a single instance in a single poem. Enjambment
represents something larger, a universal truth to which all poems
using enjambment are related synecdochically. Instead of justifying
enjambment in parts, Lawler attempts to justify it as a whole.

Williams himself shows a fondness for the universalizing approach to the technical gestures of prosody, claiming that the organization of a poem corresponds to the organization of the world
in which the poem arises. He is, however, no theoretician of enjambment, despite being one of its most avid and successful prac-
titioners. What does enjambment in his poems say about the world?
According to Lawler, enjambment is a gesture of freedom, the breaking of limits, transcendence, transformation, and union (often sexual)
with something outside oneself. Enjambment gestures from the finite
into the infinite:

> Since poetic structure is, at the least, a kind of pictogram of
> poetic statement, one would therefore expect enjambment to
> occur when assaying that situation in which, after repeated
> frustration, the human subject suddenly experiences the
> overcoming of limitations and an expansion into something
> beyond those limits.[26]

This sudden overcoming of limits in the form of endstopped lines
produces surprise: "Thus, a theory of enjambment will generally
entail a theory of poetic surprise and, with certain qualifications,
that will also be a theory of human transcendence."[27] Lawler compares the process by which enjambment generates this kind of transcendent significance to the process by which music creates meaning.
Citing Leonard Meyer as his authority, he quotes the following
passages:

> Musical meaning, then, arises when our expectant habit re-
> sponses are delayed or blocked—when the normal course of
> stylistic-mental events is disturbed by some form of deviation.
> . . . Musical meaning arises when an antecedent situation, re-
> quiring an estimate of the probable modes of pattern contin-

uation, produces uncertainty about the temporal-tonal nature
of the unexpected consequent.[28]

Affect or emotion-felt is aroused when an expectation—a
tendency to respond—activated by the musical stimulus sit-
uation, is temporarily inhibited or permanently blocked.[29]

Following Lawler's analogy, we would say that the verse line measures a course of "stylistic-mental events." Against the background
of our expectations the line does its work, delaying, disturbing,
deviating, blocking, inhibiting. In nonmetrical verse, the one-sentence, noncaesural line runs smoothly toward the fulfillment of our
expectations at the right margin. With enjambment varying degrees
of disturbance and deviation begin, bringing with them surprise,
freedom, and transcendence.

   This brief summary of Lawler's argument raises questions with
respect to Williams. In his discussion Lawler concentrates on metrical verse with a fair percentage of endstopped lines. His theory is
confirmed, for example, by this passage from "The Eve of St. Agnes":

> Beyond a mortal man impassion'd far
> At these voluptuous accents, he arose,
> Ethereal, flush'd, and like a throbbing star
> Seen mid the sapphire heaven's deep repose;
> Into her dream he melted, as the rose
> Blendeth its odour with the violet,—
> Solution sweet:                                    [XXXVI]

The strong enjambment "the rose / Blendeth" breaks the pattern of
weak phrasal enjambments and endstopped lines reinforced by rhyme.
It corresponds to a climactic moment when limits are overcome in
the act of sexual union. Rose blends with violet, man blends with
woman, the human blends with the transcendent. Surprise and freedom characterize the moment. This is, however, not often the case
with Williams's enjambments.

   In modern nonmetrical verse the limits of accentual-syllabism
have already been overcome. The endstopped line is an endangered
species. The deviations of enjambment are so common that they no
longer necessarily surprise. In poems such as "To a Poor Old Woman"

or "Seafarer" a sense of freedom and transcendence comes not with the fragmentations of enjambment, but with the release from these into the integration of line and sentence. In endstopped, accentual-syllabic verse from Chaucer through the Victorians enjambment may well function as a gesture of transcendence. In much twentieth-century enjambed, nonmetrical verse it functions more as a sign of disintegration and disconnectedness. Williams's affirmation of relativity and variability emerges in his use of line breaks that redistribute content into odd pieces. A prosody based on line-sentence counterpointing produces verse in which discord and conflict are the rule. Against this background Williams uses the endstopped line to provide a moment of rest, relief, and stability. Instead of confining, the endstopped line reassures. It is a limit we seek rather than avoid. This does not mean Williams would necessarily disagree with Lawler that in certain poems enjambment functions as a figure of freedom. Their differences begin with Williams's assumption that freedom is something the modern world often distorts and abuses. In the measured poem this freedom can be escaped.

Lawler calls poetic structure a "kind of pictogram" of poetic statement. He states positively what Dr. Johnson deplored: that enjambment is primarily a visual phenomenon. Only by seeing the enjambed poem can one understand the story lineation tells. Williams feels no more comfortable with this than Dr. Johnson. As seen in "Studiously Unprepared," he desperately wants the search for measure to lead him to the discovery of an auditory basis for the lineation of nonmetrical verse. When pressed, he acknowledges the importance of visual criteria reluctantly. In "Dartmouth College Talk" he claims that "pleasure to the [ear]" is a solid guide to line division.

In one sense, of course, it is not true that enjambment is a purely visual phenomenon. Consider five lines from *Paradise Lost* without the aid of lineation:

If answerable style I can obtain of my Celestial Patroness,
who deigns her nightly visitation unimplor'd, and dictates to
me slumb'ring, or inspires easy my unpremeditated Verse:

Like the musician or composer who can hear a piece of music and see the score in his mind, Milton's readers—or, in this case, lis-

teners—can hear the lines and visualize their arrangement. Depending on how good their ears are and how hard they listen, they know
when ten syllables and five iambic feet have gone by:

> If answerable style I can obtain
> Of my Celestial Patroness, who deigns
> Her nightly visitation unimplor'd,
> And dictates to me slumb'ring, or inspires
> Easy my unpremeditated Verse:                        [IX. 20–24]

Because these lines show an accentual-syllabic norm, the listener
can predict line breaks. He or she can hear the enjambments, as
well as see them. In the case of rhyming verse, such as the heroic
couplets of Dryden, line division and enjambment are easily audible:

> When nature prompted, and no law denied
> Promiscuous use of concubine and bride;
> Then Israel's monarch after Heaven's own heart,
> His vigorous warmth did variously impart
> To wives and slaves;
>                          ["Absalom and Achitophel," 5–9]

Without an accentual-syllabic norm, however, hearing enjambment becomes impossible. When Williams reads "Seafarer," his audience does not necessarily know that all but one of the lines have
five to eight syllables and two or three strong stresses apiece.[30] For
all it knows, the first section might look like this:

> The sea will wash in but the rocks—
> jagged ribs riding the cloth of foam
> or a knob or pinnacles with gannets—
> are the stubborn man. He invites the storm

Now the lines have eight to ten syllables each, and the passage could
pass for flexible pentameter. If Frost is correct in asserting that there
are only two meters in English—strict and loose iambic—we might
be tempted to label these lines loose blank verse.[31] As Williams reads
the poem, we can hear some of the enjambments, but by no means
all.

He usually acknowledges syntactic boundaries with a pause, slight for a comma, longer for a dash or period. The exclamation mark receives different treatment each time it appears. Where syntactic boundaries correspond to line endings, one can hear line division; yet the oral interpretation of enjambment varies throughout. Here are some notable examples:

> The sea will wash in
> but the rocks

This enjambment between two clauses of the same sentence is marked by the longest pause in the entire reading. The silence lasts three or four seconds. Although not quite as long, the next comparable pause marks a phrasal enjambment:

> or a knob or pinnacles
>     with gannets—

Here again the pause between lines seems exaggerated, as it marks the separation of a two-word prepositional phrase. On paper these enjambments are relatively low in "resistance," because they occur at major syntactic junctions, but in Williams's reading they receive the most acknowledgment. By contrast enjambments that on paper are relatively high in resistance receive no special treatment in the reading:

> He invites the storm, he
> lives by it!
>
> that inflames his blood to
> coldness
>
>             They strain
> forward to grasp ships
>
> or even the sky itself that
> bends down to be torn

These enjambments cannot be heard. Williams reads smoothly through them. One would think that the search for an auditory justification of line division would lead him to emphasize the sound of lineation in oral performance, but this is not the case. The pictogram remains only partially realized in the ear.

Wimsatt and Beardsley caution against making too much of oral performance:

> There is, of course, a sense in which the reading of the poem is primary: that is what the poem is *for*. But there is another and equally important sense in which the poem is not to be identified with any particular performance of it, or any set of such performances.[32]

In context this statement grounds an argument for the abstraction of meter from performance. With some qualification the same statement applies to enjambment. It, too, must be abstracted from oral performance. In nonmetrical verse it has no inherent auditory dimension. A given performer can attempt to dramatize the effects of lineation, but his performance presents one individual's interpretation. There is no guarantee that a given performance will successfully interpret even the most important technical gestures of a poem. As Wimsatt and Beardsley point out, this does not mean that those gestures are any less real or crucial to the overall meaning. A sequence of monosyllables in a blank verse poem may be read as spondees. An enjambment between object and preposition may sound like any other prepositional phrase.

The poem as pictogram is not just a score for performance. It includes and subsumes all performances. To semantic meanings and auditory patterns it adds a new range of visual significance. When we have the poem before us and can read it over and over, it can exploit the power of being verse to the eye. Its lines do not run together as they do in performance. Instead, each line is a discrete part we can pause over and scrutinize. Each line is a measurement not of time or syllables or accents, but of meaning. Changing the place where the line breaks changes the meaning:

> In passing with my mind
> on nothing in the world
>
> but the right of way
> I enjoyed on the road by

virtue of the law        —
I saw

an elderly man who
smiled and looked away

to the north past a house—
a woman in blue

who was laughing and
leaning forward to look up

into the man's half
averted face

and a boy of eight who was
looking at the middle of

the man's belly
at a watchchain—

The supreme importance
of this nameless spectacle

sped me by them
without a word—

Why bother where I went?
for I went spinning on the

four wheels of my car
along the wet road until

I saw a girl with one leg
over the rail of a balcony                    ["The Right of Way," *I*,
                                                          pp. 119–20]

In the prose that immediately follows this poem in *Spring and All*, Williams considers its technique:

When in the condition of imaginative suspense only will the writing have reality, as explained partially in what precedes—Not to attempt, at that time, to set values on the word

being used, according to presupposed measures, but to write
down that which happens at that time—

Williams rejects the "presupposed measures" of traditional prosody,
opting instead to use the pleasure of his ear as a solid guide to line
division. In "The Right of Way" pleasure also comes with the imaginative suspense of crossing a line boundary and seeing a one-
legged girl become a girl with two legs, one on either side of a balcony
rail. She is the emblem of enjambment, the straddler, the local genius
of the line ending who invests it with meaning, while linking one
line with the next. In her Williams sees the power to measure the
line and turn it from an abstract meter based on a uniform foot. The
foot, the measurable unit of the old line, is said to refer originally
to the rhythmic tapping of the foot, which accompanied the performance of the poem (*OED*), as, for example, the Roman soldier
set down his feet, while singing marching songs.[33] In using enjambment to break up the old line, Williams replaces the steady feet
of the marching soldier with a new metaphor: a girl with one leg
over the balcony rail and one foot in each line. She oversees the
"verse," the turn (*versus*) from one line into another.[34] When Williams
asserts that verse must be measured, he restores the original metaphor: measure the *versus* by regulating its resistance; take pleasure
in it and forget the tapping foot. The marching soldier embodied
regularity, predictability, and discipline, as he established an empire
and brought pleasure to his era. Williams, however, no longer finds
pleasure in the march. Instead, he turns to the girl on the balcony
for guidance. Along the road where soldiers marched the poet drives
his car. When he looks up, she is there pointing out the right of
way.

# The Field of Daisies:
# Visual Prosody and
# Typographic Inscription

Good Christ what is
a poet—if any
            exists?

a man
whose words will
        bite
                their way
home—being actual

having the form
            of motion

      —"The Wind Increases"

Williams's struggle with the question of how "free" verse is measured
led him to experiment with the visual patterns of poetry. In a poem
without an accentual-syllabic standard of measurement the importance of these patterns increases. In discussing "Seafarer," I noted
several instances of line division, their various effects, and possible
meanings; yet the poem has a prominent typographic feature which
remains to be analyzed. It appears in the first section or stanza:

The sea will wash in
but the rocks—jagged ribs
riding the cloth of foam
or a knob or pinnacles

> with gannets—
> are the stubborn man.                    [*CLP*, p. 170]

The fifth line, shortest in the poem with three syllables, is displaced from the left margin well towards the right. It is the only such line in "Seafarer." The reason for this indentation is not immediately apparent. Because the poem shows no recurrent tendency towards variability in the left margin, this one indentation seems anomalous. It does not represent any striking shift or development in thematic content; the prepositional phrase "with gannets" would not otherwise arouse much speculation. With the indentation, however, we cannot help but wonder: Is this an arbitrary move on Williams's part? Is he calling attention to the shortest line in "Seafarer," choosing to align it, more or less, with the right margin rather than the left? Recalling Pound's free translation of "The Seafarer" from Anglo-Saxon, we might opt for more subtle interpretation. Because the gannet (Old English: *ganot*) appears in both the original poem and Pound's translation, perhaps the indentation marks the point where Williams's poem contacts the work of his contemporary and, through him, poetic tradition.

Speculation becomes more complicated when we consult the first printing of "Seafarer" in *Interim*.[1] Originally titled "The Sea Farer," the poem opens this way:

> The sea will wash in
> and the rocks—whether seen
> by air, jagged ribs
> riding the cloth of foam
> or a knob or pinnacles
> lined with gannets—
> whose screams we may guess,
> are the stubborn man.

There is no break after the last line, the poem forming instead a solid column. Here none of the lines is indented. Instead of "with gannets" we have "lined with gannets." Allowing for differences in typesetting, we see that the blank space in the later version is approximately the length of the canceled word "lined." In the case of a poet preoccupied with the line—its measurement, division, and arrangement—it does seem odd that this should be the missing word. Unlike other differences between the two versions—the cancellations of "whether seen / by air" and "whose screams we may guess," and the replacement of "and" with "but" in the second line—the substitution of blank space for "lined" does not yield readily to analysis. Was it a printer's error? Did Williams cancel the word "lined" on the page proof, intending to replace it with something else, but later forget?

This second question is particularly interesting, because it imagines Williams's poem reenacting the origin of paragraph indentation. In the history of printing, according to Jan Tschichold, paragraph indentation began with omission:

> The early printers always marked their paragraphs, usually with the paragraph sign [here the sign appears] hand-drawn in red. A space was left for the sign. Often it was never drawn in and before long the space alone was sufficient to mark the paragraph.[2]

A page of prose would have appeared as a solid block of print with blank spaces scattered through it, each awaiting a paragraph sign. (The etymological meaning of "paragraph" is "beside sign," i.e., the sign that is drawn beside.) Eventually, after these signs were no longer used, the spaces themselves were set at the left margin, giving the page an appearance of neat regularity. Spaces in printed prose, which were originally blanks left to be filled in, came to signify divisions in content. These divisions are marked by indentations.

The principle of paragraph indentation, which originates in the typography of prose, finds its way into the typography of poetry with verse paragraphing. In Williams's poetry the verse paragraph appears first in *The Tempers* (1913; "The Death of Franco of Cologne: His Prophecy of Beethoven"). With *Al Que Quiere!* (1917) the verse paragraph takes its place beside the other patterns, stanzaic and nonstanzaic, which occur throughout Williams's work. It appears frequently in *Collected Earlier Poems, Collected Later Poems,* and *Paterson* but vanishes with *Pictures from Brueghel,* which is dominated by regularity, both stanzaic (*Pictures from Brueghel*) and triadic (*The Desert Music; Journey to Love*). The verse paragraph, however, does not account for all the spaces and indentations in Williams's poems. Whatever its origin, in "Seafarer" the indented line does not represent the beginning of a new paragraph; it breaks the pattern of left-justified lines. In so doing, it sets off the prepositional phrase "with gannets," isolating a single visual detail from the rest of the poem. The gannets, the only living creatures in the poem aside from the speaker, stand out in his vision—and ours—from the rest of the scene. The act of indenting one line gives that line significance as both a thematic and typographic entity.

Williams's use of indentation precedes his discovery of verse paragraphing. Of the twenty-six poems in *Poems* (1909), fifteen of which are sonnets, four show indentation patterns. Of the twenty-eight poems in *The Tempers* (*CEP*), twelve show indentation patterns. Unlike "Seafarer," however, these poems indent lines at predictable points for obvious reasons. The short poem "Mezzo Forte" is an example:

> Take that, damn you; and that!
>     And here's a rose
>   To make it right again!
>     God knows
>   I'm sorry, Grace; but then,
> It's not my fault if you will be a cat.        [*CEP*, p. 21]

In this poem, whose title states that it should be "played" moderately, indentation corresponds to rhyme. The first and sixth lines rhyme; they are left-justified. The third and fifth lines rhyme; they are indented slightly. The second and fourth lines rhyme; they are indented farthest. Indentation also corresponds to line length: the shortest lines indented farthest, longer lines indented slightly, longest lines left-justified. (In this case line length also works with an iambic norm.) The rigid typographic patterning contrasts sharply with the informality of tone and diction. The effect is humorous. "Mezzo Forte," played half loud, needs to be read half seriously.

In using indentation this way, Williams follows the typographic conventions of English poetry before the Romantics. Indentations signify auditory phenomena. Lines indented the same distance usually rhyme or are metrically similar, or both. The typography of ballads, sapphics, elegiacs, and some sonnets demonstrates these conventions. Even the unique stanzas of such poets as Skelton, Donne, and Herbert follow this pattern, although the indentations often reflect meter alone, rather than rhyme and meter together. Given that the right margin varies slightly, poems using indentation this way appear to be centered, symmetric, and regular. In surveying the history of typography, Tschichold analyzes symmetric or "axial" typography as follows:

> In centered typography, pure form comes before the meaning
> of the words. . . . The canon of beauty was the human body
> and its proportions were applied to every problem of design.[3]

The statement "pure form comes before the meaning of the words" presents some questions. Presumably a poet could manipulate his poem so that form and meaning would coincide. If he wanted to isolate a particular group of words, he could place them in a short line indented farthest from the left, as Donne and Herbert often do. With this qualification, however, Tschichold's claim seems valid. Once Donne decided to write "The Canonization" and worked out an appropriate stanza pattern, he did not permit himself typographic freedoms such as this:

> For God's sake hold your tongue, and let me love,
>    Or chide my palsy, or my gout,
> My five
>
>      gray
>    hairs, or ruined fortune, flout,
> With wealth your state, your mind with arts improve
>     Take you a course, get you a place,
>     Observe His Honor, or His Grace,
> Or the King's real, or his stamped face
>    Contemplate; what you will, approve,
>    So you will let me love.

No matter how much those gray hairs meant to him, Donne would not violate the symmetry of his stanzas. If the canon of beauty is the human body, the poet may not place a foot where a hand should

be. Among modern poets Marianne Moore composed many poems
with stanzas that reveal the same combination of eccentric indentation patterns and strict symmetry found in English metaphysical
poetry. In his early indented poems Williams follows the laws of
symmetric typography as they pertain to the printing of poetry,
although unlike Donne, Herbert, or Moore, he does not interpret
those laws adventurously. In "Hic Jacet," for example, one of seven
poems published in *The Poetry Review* in October 1912, the indentation pattern corresponds to rhyme scheme:

> The coroner's merry little children
>     Have such twinkling brown eyes.
> Their father is not of gay men
>     And their mother jocular in no wise,
> Yet the coroner's merry little children
>         Laugh so easily.
>
> They laugh because they prosper.
>     Fruit for them is upon all branches.
> Lo! how they jibe at loss, for
>     Kind heaven fills their little paunches!
> It's the coroner's merry, merry children
>         Who laugh so easily.                    [*CEP*, p. 30]

Here Williams rhymes "prosper" with "loss, for," pairing a disyllable
with two monosyllables and an endstopped line with an enjambed
one. The detachment of the subordinate clause "Kind heaven fills
their little paunches!" from its conjunction "for" disrupts the predictable verse scheme at a moment when irony swerves into the
grotesqueness of black humor. In its context, the technique is effective; yet by comparison with the complex network of indentations
and enjambments in Moore's "The Fish," it is also slight.

But the Romantic poets did not invent verse paragraphing; it
appears, for example, throughout *Paradise Lost*. Having indented the
first line of a new paragraph, Milton ends that paragraph with a full
pentameter line. The same is true of Dryden and Pope: a new paragraph begins with an indented line only after the old paragraph
closes with a full pentameter. The typography looks like this:

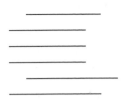

Indentation here, as in prose, corresponds to content, not to rhyme or meter. The spatial arrangement, though noticeable, does not produce any striking effect. But the Romantics give this arrangement a twist: the new paragraph with its indentation may occur within a line rather than between lines, recalling the technique, used by Elizabethan dramatists, of changing speakers in the middle of a pentameter line. When this happens, the first line of the new paragraph is indented under or just beyond the last line of the old paragraph, producing this sort of arrangement:

> With some uncertain notice, as might seem
> Of vagrant dwellers, in the houseless woods,
> Or of some Hermit's cave, where by his fire
> The Hermit sits alone.
>
>       These beauteous forms,
> Through a long absence, have not been to me
> As is a landscape to a blind man's eye:

The full pentameter is now broken into two parts, the last line of the old paragraph and the first line of the new. Each part is partially framed by blank space, setting it off from the lines above or below it. In a note to "Tintern Abbey," from which this example is taken, Wordsworth interprets his arrangement: "I have not ventured to call this Poem an Ode; but it was written with a hope that in the transitions and the impassioned music of the versification, would be found the principal requisites, of that species of composition."[4] The radical indentations let space into the verse column at irregular intervals, signaling the abrupt discontinuities and shifts associated with the Romantic ode. Unlike *Paradise Lost*, "Tintern Abbey" uses verse paragraphing to dramatize the emotional operations of a speaker's mind rather than to indicate the logic of narrative sequence or rational argument.

Williams may have discovered the Romantic verse paragraph in his reading of Keats, who uses it throughout "Endymion."[5] He may have learned of it from Pound, who uses it, for example, in his version of "The Seafarer" (1912). Wherever he first came across it, Williams found in this technique a typographic format more to his liking than the symmetric typography of conventionally indented poems. With the Romantic verse paragraph the possibilities of asymmetric typography begin to unfold. In *Al Que Quiere!* (*CEP*) at least sixteen of the forty-nine poems use indentation in ways that suggest Romantic verse paragraphing. In some cases this results in the placement of only one or two lines well toward the right margin. The poems tend to divide sharply at these points. As special instances of this phenomenon Williams sometimes closes poems with a short "paragraph":

> No one
> will believe this
> of vast import to the nation.         ["Pastoral"; *CEP*, p. 121]

> These things
> astonish me beyond words.         ["Pastoral"; *CEP*, p. 124]

> Go now
> I think you are ready.         ["Tract"; *CEP*, p. 131]

In each case the indented line marks the transition into a sort of coda, a generalization or observation detached from the poem both typographically and thematically. Each of the indented lines contains two one-syllable words, and two of the three are enjambed, with subjects dividing from predicates. In the example from "Tract" the absence of endstopping punctuation after "Go now" produces what we might call "pseudo-enjambment," because it causes the reader to expect continuation beyond the line ending, as in "Go now / and begin." The combination of indentation and enjambment intensifies our perception of each word pair. "No one," "These things," "Go now"—these phrases stand out on the page. In the first example, the detached phrase also functions as a synecdoche, concentrating a larger meaning from the poem into a small typographic node.

Asymmetric typography allows distinctions in meaning that symmetric typography does not. Of course symmetric typography produces arrangements that have their own meaning. A stanza, verse block, or verse column—each has an identity we recognize and assimilate before we begin reading. Symmetric formats appear throughout Williams's work; they may even constitute a majority. In *Sour Grapes* (1921), for example, only three of the poems use verse paragraphing. Instead, stanzas, verse blocks, and verse columns dominate, their left-justified lines giving an impression of compact neatness. With *Spring and All* (1923) experiments in asymmetric typography become more prominent. Williams's comments on that book reveal an emerging self-consciousness: "It was written when all the world was going crazy about typographical form and is really a travesty on the idea."[6] Five years before the appearance of *Spring and All* Guillaume Apollinaire published his *Calligrammes* containing several early twentieth-century examples of concrete poetry. Two years after Williams's book appeared, Jan Tschichold introduced the "new typography" to the world in *Elementare Typographie* (Leipzig, 1925), a special issue of a periodical he was then editing. Typographic experimentation emerged in America with Cummings's first book, *Tulips and Chimneys*, published the same year as *Spring and All*. In light of all this innovation, Williams's own experiments seem modest, especially for a travesty: poetry mixed with prose, some irregular prose paragraphing, a sprinkling of boldface print, a chapter heading set upside down and a few moves like these:

> petals radiant with transpiercing light
> contending
>
>            above
>
> the leaves
> reaching up their modest green
> from the pot's rim                              [*SA*, II]
>
> I was your nightgown
>        I       watched!          [*SA*, IX][7]

Of the twenty-seven poems in *Spring and All* (twenty-eight in *CEP*), twenty-two consist entirely of left-justified lines. Fourteen are arranged symmetrically into stanzas, including "The Red Wheelbarrow." In the few examples of asymmetric typography that we do have, spatial displacements are no longer confined to the indentations of verse paragraphing, although they may reflect an extension of that principle. Williams apparently had second thoughts about his travesty, as neither of the examples above is printed exactly this way in *CEP*. In the first case "above" is the only displaced line in the poem, as is "with gannets" in "Seafarer." In the second "I        watched!" is one of three indented lines, but occurs near the end of a three-page poem, the other two at the beginning. The temptation is to say that the spatial isolation of "above," "I," and "watched" emphasizes these words. This can be misleading. Typography does not emphasize a word or group of words the way that italicization and underscoring do; it does not guide the reader toward stress or intonation, performed or imagined. If we reprinted these lines to read "with transpiercing light / contending *above* the leaves" or "I was your nightgown / *I watched*," we would produce different effects. The emphasis on "above" would distinguish it from "below." The emphasis on "I watched" might signal the urgency of confession or voyeuristic ecstasy, as opposed to the strange understatement of human consciousness projected onto a piece of clothing.

Typographic isolation does not "emphasize"; it frames, rendering a familiar word or phrase momentarily unfamiliar. Instead of emphasizing a word toward a particular significance, spatial displacement strips it of familiar associations with words around it, associations on which simple emphasis depends. Emphasis limits the range of possible meanings. Typography breaks those limits. In this way typography performs some of the same work as enjambment, although typography often does it more effectively. In a poem where enjambment is the norm, one can read through a given instance without attaching particular significance to it. It is difficult, however, to read unconsciously through the examples above. In the first case the displacement of "above" breaks in—"amidst transpiercing radiance"—on the visual observation of pink and white flowers. The moment is epiphanic. Above is more than the opposite of below; it is the direction of transcendence. The possibility that "above" is an adverb lingers after it descends into prepositionalism, toward the leaves and the moss. In *Spring and All*, II, typography intensifies a particular moment in the poem, a moment when observation is suspended in revelation.

Visiting Italy in 1924, Williams encountered the typographic experiments of the Futurist poets, such as those published in the magazines *Lacerba* (Florence, 1913–15) and *La Voce* (Florence, 1908–16), as well as in F. T. Marinetti's anthology *I nuovi poeti futuristi* (Rome, 1925). In the improvisation "Rome" (1924) he notes his reaction to these experiments:

> this is what writers have always tried to show by what they term form, to show it is different in substance from prose. it is the same writers try today to indicate by the irregular spacing and capitalization of letters, size position on a page as can be seen from the American Cummings to the Hungarian Kassak, lines. rhymes: to indicate something else besides (the prose sense) what is written (which poetry uses also) this is a valuable adjunct to poetry but of no material significance—if the same end of radiant motion can be won by a simpler expedient—[8]

Poetic form indicates something else besides "the prose sense." Typographic format, or shape, is only one aspect of formal structure, but in some verse, such as Cummings's, it emerges as the dominant one. In "Rome" Williams considers this "a valuable adjunct to poetry but of no material significance—if the same end of radiant motion can be won by a simpler expedient." The phrase "radiant motion" seems to refer to large and luminous aspects of the poem, both formal and thematic. At this point Williams apparently considers typographic format extraneous to the poetic form of radiant motion. Nevertheless, he continued to experiment with the visual surface of his poems.

In *The Descent of Winter* (1928) symmetric and asymmetric typography are about evenly represented. Neither is the rule, neither the exception. Left-justified stanzas ("9/29"; "9/30"; "10/9"), conventional indentation patterns ("10/29"; "11/20"), verse paragraphs ("A Morning Imagination of Russia"), and irregular arrangements ("10/28"; "10/30"; "11/2") all make their appearance. Although Williams

does not "go crazy" over typographic form, he apparently no longer
feels the need to travesty the idea. Throughout the thirties and forties
he continued to use asymmetric typography before returning to
symmetric formats in the last decade of his career. "Della Primavera
Transportata al Morale" (1934), "The Pink Church" (1946), "The
Desert Music" (1951), and parts of *Paterson* (1946–58) are examples
of Williams's more remarkable explorations into the possibilities of
asymmetric typography. The shorter poem "The Wind Increases,"
first published in *An Early Martyr* (1935), embodies some of the same
techniques:

> The harried
> earth is swept
>                       The trees
> the tulip's bright
>         tips
>                       sidle and
> toss—
>
>         Loose your love
> to flow
>
> Blow!
>
> Good Christ what is
> a poet—if any
>                       exists?
>
> a man
> whose words will
>         bite
>                       their way
> home—being actual
>
> having the form
>                       of motion
>
> At each twigtip
>
> new
>
> upon the tortured

> body of thought
>           gripping
>    the ground
>
> a way
>           to the last leaftip                    [*CEP*, pp. 68–69]

It is not a matter here of discussing one or two displaced lines in a poem otherwise loyal to the left margin. Asymmetry, irregularity, indentation, and variation sweep the poem as "The harried / earth is swept." Despite its windblown appearance, however, the poem has boundaries within which typographic dispersion is contained. The widest strip of print on the page appears at the close of the poem: "a way / to the last leaftip." This amounts to seven syllables and twenty-four spaces on a typewriter—about half the length of the longest lines in "The Yachts," published in the same year. Falling within this limit, the rest of the lines sketch a column, albeit a column perforated with blank spaces. Pressing towards a representational theory of typographic form, we might say that the irregular column of type suggests a tree trunk or a flower stem moving with the wind. Six years before the appearance of "The Wind Increases" Williams published "Rain," a poem in which the scattering of single words and phrases down the page mimes the falling of individual raindrops. Although not so obviously, a similar impulse towards pictorial representation may be working in the later poem.

Typography does not establish all the patterns in "The Wind Increases." An iambic tendency surfaces occasionally:

The hárried eárth is swépt

a mán whose wórds will bíte their wáy

Various auditory patterns also emerge, among them the recurrence of the long "o": flow, blow, poet, home, motion. Finally, there is the rhetorical structure of the content itself. Beginning and ending with images of windswept flora, "The Wind Increases" centers on a statement about the poet, a statement set in the form of question and answer:

       Good Christ what is
       a poet—if any
                         exists?

       a man
       whose words will
             bite
                         their way
       home—being actual

       having the form
                   of motion

A poet is someone whose words bite the way a sharp wind bites. In this equation Williams draws on the association of wind with *spiritus*, the divine breath of inspiration; yet he focuses on a particular aspect of the analogy. A poet is not just someone with an imagination upon which inspiration plays like wind on an Aeolian harp. For Williams the poet is someone who moves through words, giving them "the form / of motion," as the wind moves through the trees and flowers. The phrase "the form of motion" is particularly significant. "Motion" could be a metaphor for the movement of reality through the imagination and the imagination through reality, as in the "radiant motion" mentioned in "Rome." One "form" of this motion is art, and one form of art is poetry, which uses words to describe the interpenetrating motions of imagination and reality. The words of a poem are the form of these motions.

A second reading of "the form of motion" interprets the phrase somewhat differently. Williams's statements about poetry often lead to temporal theories of prosody; to measure the line is to measure the time of the line, he insists. In "The Wind Increases," however, time is not the issue; motion is. Of course time and motion cannot be separated. The measurement of time depends on the movement of the earth in relation to the sun. When we perceive motion, we perceive it occurring in space through time. A poet's words do not literally move. They are fixed on the page and cannot change position the way words can in movie credits or television commercials. Through the arrangement of words on a page, however, the poet can give his words the "form" of motion. He can arrange them to represent rain falling or some other motion he sees in the world, as Cummings often does, such as in his poems about a grasshopper jumping ("r-p-o-p-h-e-s-s-a-g-r") or a leaf falling ("1(a").[9] He can also use typography to represent more abstract motions of thought and attention. "The Wind Increases" is not simply a poem arranged to look as though the wind is blowing it around; it is also a poem about typography and how typography can be used to trace the path the mind takes as it swells from breeze to gale. The violence done by asymmetric typography both to stanzas or columns and to the syntactic sequences within them corresponds to a violence within the "tortured / body of thought," the violence of anything new: a passion, an idea, a season between now and the end, the "last leaftip." Asymmetric typography keeps the poem moving across the page, never letting it settle. Just when a pattern seems to be emerging, it is torn apart. The poem rejects the steadiness of couplets four times, as each of four pairs of left-justified lines gives way immediately to irregular indentation and spacing. Each rejection is both an act of mind and typography, a motion of the body of thought enacted by words on the page, those words "being actual."

Any poem printed on a page in lines that are not justified at both margins shows a typographic format which can be analyzed as a visual organization of space. To some this is no more significant a statement than saying that every poem is made of words. Charles Hartman, for example, asserts that verse is primarily a "temporal medium," although the experiments of Cummings and the concrete poets represent verse in which the "spatial element" in poetry assumes a greater importance.[10] Wimsatt is more severe in his criticism of what he calls "merely typographical measures" through which "poetry merely attempts to become a visual art." As examples he lists the *technopaignia*, or shaped poems of classical tradition, Apollinaire's *Calligrammes*, the syllabics of Marianne Moore, some of the poems of Cummings, and the "column-width" lines of William Carlos Williams.[11] Finally, John Sparrow in his work on epigraphy differentiates between a Latin inscription and the "Easter Wings" of George Herbert or Apollinaire's *Calligrammes* by describing the latter this way: "Writing of this kind is not inscriptional, because the visual form does not contribute to the meaning of the text, but merely illustrates it; such examples are simply a kind of visual pun."[12] These are strong statements. In contesting them, we would need to consider the metaphysics of a space-time continuum; we might wonder how the visual arts evolved into something poetry "merely" attempts to become; we could argue that anything which illustrates meaning necessarily contributes to it, and that the pun in particular produces meaning in a way that nothing else can. These debates, however, could not solve basic difficulties.

In arguing for the importance of typography to the study of verse, one can easily slip into defense and overanalysis of the seemingly trivial: the number of spaces a line is indented, the variability of margination, the significance of boldface print. Looking in the indices of most studies or handbooks of prosody will not yield entries for these things. After all, what matters more is what Spenser "says" in his *Faerie Queene*, not the fact that he supervised the printing of the poem, insisting that the first and ninth lines of his stanzas be left-justified and the middle seven indented. Even the stanza patterns our eyes recognize are, or are descended from, maps for the ear, guiding us through rhyme schemes, syllable counts, and accent patterns. One can speculate that the effects of television, film, videotape, and the computer may shift this balance in the next century, but that remains speculation.

In Williams's poetry typography plays a complicated role. As usual his own comments on the subject are contradictory. In an undated, unpublished fragment called "Verse caligrams" [*sic*] he makes the following statement disguised as a prescription:

> Divide it (the page and the words on it) in any way you please, in any neat form you choose.
>
> BUT learn to measure the line. Then the measured line need not in the least conform to the visual convenience on the page. The true decipherer will know the divisions—but the others will read their verse and never know the difference.[13]

The title and tone of this statement suggest a dig at Apollinaire, over whose typographic innovations the world was going crazy in

1918 instead of *Al Que Quiere!* Williams dismisses typography as something of secondary importance compared to the measurement of the individual line. In a sense, of course, he's right. "The true decipherer" can hear iambs throughout "The Wind Increases," despite its "neat form." Presumably he would also have no trouble deciphering the true measure of this arrangement:

> This is the forest
>
> primeval
> the murmuring
>          pines and the
>
>    hemlocks

Here Longfellow's single measured line does not conform to the "visual convenience" on the page. His dactylic march, or perhaps our familiarity with that march, transcends lineation.

    What happens, however, when, try as he will, the true decipherer can decipher no true pattern of line measurement? Williams's so-called two-stress line has a tenuous hold on accentual measure, but that hold depends entirely on lineation. Before she offers another scansion of her own, Linda Wagner shows how the following lines from "Good Night" might be considered two-stress by some readers:

> In brilliant gas light
> I turn the kitchen spigot
> and watch the water plash
> into the clean white sink.             [*CEP*, p. 145][14]

This scansion depends on the principle of relative stress: within a given line two syllables receive stronger stress relative to the other syllables in the line. Breaking up the line breaks up the two-stress pattern:

> In brilliant gas light I turn the
> kitchen spigot and watch the water
> plash into the clean white sink.

In brilliant gas
light I turn the
kitchen spigot and
watch the water
plash
into the clean
white sink.

    In brilliant
                    gas light
    I turn
    the kitchen
                    spigot
    and watch
    the water plash
                    into
    the
        clean white sink.

What has happened to the true two-stress measure in these examples?
If anything, it seems that a solid iambic base ("I turn the kitchen
spigot / and watch the water plash") is what shows through the
various typographic arrangements; yet, if Williams wanted us to feel
a two-stress measure, how would that measure survive these typographic rearrangements? It wouldn't. Here measurement depends
on the neat form of lineation; it is not inherently strong enough to
transcend typography.

Williams considers this problem of the role typography plays in
measuring verse in the following statement:

> What else is verse made of but "words, words, words"? Quite
> literally, *the spaces between the words*, in our modern under-
> standing, which takes with them an equal part in the measure.[15]

The spaces between words are purely typographic features. In speech
itself elision and contraction prevent hearing spaces between words.
These spaces, however, now contribute to the measurement of verse.
This is a late statement by Williams, drafted in the fall and winter
of 1958–59. His experiments with the variable foot, in which the

spacing of words into lines and lines into triads is primary, lay behind him. Attempting to decipher what Williams meant by the assertion that spaces between words take "an equal part" in the measure, Mary Ellen Solt explains that in the triadic line poems spaces represent pauses.[16] If this were true, the space created by indentation or skipping a line would correspond to a rest in music. Typographic spaces would serve as temporal ciphers. Given Williams's love of time-based prosody, he may well have meant something like this; yet, as with other features of his pseudo-quantitative theory, this presents problems for a reader. Because the third line of a triadic stanza is indented twice as far as the second, do we infer that it represents a pause two times as long? How do we begin to translate the spaces in "The Wind Increases" or *Spring and All* into time? Rather than say a space equals a rest in an abstract temporal scheme, Williams might have said that typographic spacing gives a sense of rest within a visual field. The figure comes from painting instead of music, and the page becomes a canvas rather than a musical score.

Williams's relationship to the visual arts, especially painting, has been widely studied and discussed.[17] He painted briefly and considered becoming a painter, as his mother was. His painting of a scene along the Passaic River (*circa* 1912) and his self-portrait (1914) have been reproduced in several books. He went to the Armory Show in 1913. He knew the painters and photographers of the New York avant-garde. His intense consciousness of modern art is not disputed. What can be questioned is the role that consciousness plays in the techniques of Williams's poetry. One could say, with Wimsatt, that Williams merely attempted to make poetry a visual art. Or, one could argue that the influence of modern art on Williams shows in his handling of visual detail, point of view, temporal sequence, and conceptual organization. Such a view produces convincing readings of individual poems, such as Whittemore's interpretation of "The Young Housewife" as a cubist poem.[18]

Whittemore divides "The Young Housewife" into four "planes" which would be mixed on the surface of a canvas. This reading is appealing not only because it imports the metaphors of painting into poetry, but also because it hints at one of the reasons behind Williams's attraction to cubism: the poet with a time-based prosody feels a kinship with a movement whose works call into question our perception of temporal sequence. Whittemore's reading, however, interprets the relationship between painting and poetry figuratively. When he, like Dijkstra, invites us to see the poem as a canvas, he means for us to read through its thematic content using the categories of painting. He does not mean that we should let our eyes tell us that "The Young Housewife" has three stanzas of four, five, and three lines, all of which are left-justified, and is not particularly striking in its typographic format. Williams, however, saw his poems this way, if his published comments are any indication. The categories of visual art pertain to his poetry both figuratively and literally.

In his essay "E. E. Cummings's Paintings and Poems" (1954), Williams shows how he brings these categories to his analysis of Cummings's short poem "nonsun blob a":

> nonsun blob a
> cold to
> skylessness
> sticking fire
>
> my are your
> are birds our all
> and one gone
> away the they
>
> leaf of ghosts some
> few creep there
> here or on
> unearth[19]

What in the world are you to make of this poem? Because when you are a critic you are definitely not a poet. I'll show you.

It is, definitely, a composition (a conventional composition)—it has to be for the lines are arranged regularly. In fact they are arranged in the form of a quatrain: four lines followed by four lines. That is always something.

Each of these groups of four lines is followed by another to which it is similar. In what is it similar to the one that precedes it? It is like the one that precedes it in the organization of its rhythmical sequence; that is what (musically) it means. Poems are like that.

*Therefore* it is a poem and not for anything the lines *say*.

It is thrilling thus to have the lines reft of sense and returned to music.

It is marvelous to be so intoxicatedly loosed along the page. We (as all poets feel) are free to cut diagonally across the page as if it were a field of daisies to lie down among them when the sun is shining "to loaf at our ease."[20]

The poem is a poem because it is arranged in lines, and the lines are arranged symmetrically in stanzas. Thematic content is put aside. The typographic arrangement establishes a regular rhythm, a measure. Williams chooses to call this rhythm musical, but the rhythm is in fact visual. The strongest pattern in Cummings's poem emerges through lineation, not through auditory phenomena. The quatrains here are fossil forms, rhyme and meter having died out from them. Still, they are forms, and those forms are sufficient, at least in Williams's mind, to do the work of measuring Cummings's poem. We can imagine that Williams's own analysis of "The Young Housewife" would be similar. The difference between his poem and Cummings's is that the latter has three symmetric quatrains, whereas in the former one line has migrated from the third quatrain up to the second, disrupting perfect symmetry. The rhythm established by the first quatrain varies in the second and third.

Given the strict regularity of Cummings's visual format, it seems odd that Williams should suddenly begin rhapsodizing about the feeling of being so "intoxicatedly loosed along the page." Perhaps he means that syllabic and accentual restrictions have been lifted in favor of typographic ones. But when he speaks of the freedom "to cut diagonally across the page as if it were a field of daisies," he is not speaking of this poem by Cummings. Instead, he seems to be celebrating his own triadic stanza in a burst of Whitmanian exuberance. The allusion to the opening lines of "Song of Myself" has an ironic twist to it. Although Whitman is the father of American free verse and the patron saint of loafers, typography plays a limited part in his poetry. Through hundreds of pages of verse visual format varies little. A notable exception is "O Captain! My Captain!" which closes this way:

> Exult O shores, and ring O bells!
>   But I with mournful tread,
>     Walk the deck my Captain lies,
>       Fallen cold and dead.

Here Whitman does a little diagonal loafing of his own, cutting a path across the field of daisies for the triadic line to follow one hundred years later.

A purely graphic theory of prosodic measurement has inevitable limitations. Because the ear dominates prosodic theory, auditory phenomena will continue to take precedence in the writing and ana-lyzing of verse. Someone has yet to say that all poetry aspires to the condition of painting. Where auditory patterns are strong, typography will be considered secondary. Where auditory patterns are weak, poetry will be accused of being prose. Many readers feel that strong visual patterns do not compensate for the loss of rhyme schemes and scansions. Still, if we do not attempt to universalize a theory of graphic prosody, reserving it instead for poets who show strong visual orientation, we may begin to differentiate among those poets. The poets of the *technopaignia*, George Herbert, Guillaume Apolli-naire, Marianne Moore, E. E. Cummings, and William Carlos Wil-liams cannot be lumped into the group "visual poets" and dismissed as aberrations, having been explained. Instead, the visual arrange-ments these poets produce can be divided into two basic categories: those that are mimetic representations of visible phenomena in the world and those that are not. For the sake of convenience we might call this latter category "abstract," as poems belonging to it use typography to explore the spatial relations of words, lines, and groups of lines to each other, not to external shapes and forms.

The distinction between abstract and representational formats is not always a clear one. In one sense every format is representational. On the page a sonnet represents an ideal auditory form that has one hundred and forty syllables, seventy of which are stressed, and a certain number of rhymes, depending on the sonnet form. It is a picture of sound, as is a graph of soundwave measurements. It is not, however, a mimetic representation of something else we have seen with our eyes: a pair of wings (Herbert), rain falling (Apollinaire, Williams), or a grasshopper's flight (Cummings). These acts of typographic mimesis produce the visual puns that Sparrow differentiates from inscriptions. With the exception of "Rain" and possibly "The Wind Increases," Williams did not produce poems of this sort.[21] One of his poems, however, might be classified as belonging to a rarefied form of typographic mimesis. Along with poems about wings in the shape of wings, here is a poem about the quatrain in the shape of two quatrains:

THE DISH OF FRUIT

The table describes
nothing: four legs, by which
it becomes a table. Four lines
by which it becomes a quatrain,

the poem that lifts the dish
of fruit, if we say it is like
a table—how will it describe
the contents of the poem?                              [*CLP*, p. 91]

This is a special form of mimesis. Related to the family of sonnets on the sonnet (by Wordsworth, Keats, Rossetti), "The Dish of Fruit" might be considered an example of "self-reflexive" mimesis: it represents itself. Like "Easter Wings" it is a visual pun; yet the mimesis continues beyond the simple equation of visual format with thematic content. The quatrain is a picture of a quatrain, but it is also a picture of a table, albeit a crude one, each line representing a leg. On top of that table (quatrain) rests a dish of fruit. The poet before his quatrain stands like any one of all the painters who have stood before dishes of fruit on tables, preparing to paint still lifes. The question the poem poses is a difficult one: How will the poem that is shaped like a table (quatrain) describe its own contents? How does visual format combine with thematic content to produce meaning? If Sparrow is correct, when the format puns on content, it merely illustrates. It merely supports the dish of fruit. "The Dish of Fruit," however, is not just a pun; it is a meditation on the typography of verse. Williams's question might also be paraphrased, How does lineation contribute to meaning when the line performs as a typographic entity?

The basic material of typography is a line of language. Where a single word appears isolated, it will be considered a one-word line. As Tschichold remarks, "All typography is an arrangement of elements in two dimensions."[22] In this respect typography is like painting. If an arrangement produces a mimetic representation, that is one thing. If it does not, it still produces lines which are shapes that exist on the page in relation to each other and the space around them.[23] This relation is the focus of "abstract" typography. Unlike abstract art, abstract typography does not use color or shapes other than the shapes of words in lines. Tschichold explores the analogy between art and typography further:

> The connection between "abstract" painting and the new typography does not lie in the use of "abstract" forms but in the similarity of working methods. In both, the artist must first make a scientific study of his available materials and then, using contrast, forge them into an entity. All abstract paintings, especially "quite simple" ones, contain artistic or graphic elements which besides being clearly defined themselves also have a clear relationship to each other. From here the step to typography is a short one. The works of "abstract" art are subtle creations of order out of simple contrasting elements. Because this is exactly what typography is trying to do, it can derive stimulus and instruction from a study of such paintings, which communicate the visual forms of the modern world and are the best teachers of visual order.[24]

The language of this passage might well have appealed to Williams, its emphasis on order corresponding to his insistence on measure. When rhyme, meter, syllable counts, and stanza patterns have all been stripped away from verse, one can still produce "subtle creations of order out of simple contrasting elements," those elements being lines of language.[25] In turn, these subtle creations of order, although they may have no obvious mimetic value, certainly have expressive significance. The fact that typography uses language in lines also differentiates it from painting. If typography did nothing but arrange lines of letters randomly chosen, it might deserve the charge of "merely" attempting to do what other forms of visual art do much more effectively. Because abstract typography organizes language in lines, it produces not only subtle creations of visual order, but also subtle creations of thematic order. These creations of thematic order may be considered inscriptional.

The painter in Williams may have intuited the ordering, measuring power of typography, but the poet in him insisted on describing this power in terms borrowed from music. Spaces between words had to be musical rests. The rhythm established by three quatrains on a page had to be musical rhythm. Typography had to be something travestied before it was grudgingly acknowledged. In seeking to justify his own experiments in free verse, Williams struggled hard to align himself with prosodic theories that are not equipped to discuss poetry as a visual art. Admittedly, there is no reason they should be, because poetry is not primarily a visual art; it is a verbal one. Verse written in English does not have the same inherent visual quality that Chinese verse does, although English letters derive from ideographs. A Chinese ideogram is already a mimetic representation, or, as Fenollosa claims, "a vivid shorthand picture of the operations of nature."[26] On several pages of the *Cantos* Pound achieves a special visual effect by importing these mimetic representations into the midst of his own abstract typography. The ideograms, as fusions of the verbal and visual, sanction the typographic arrangements around them. Pound's reader sees in the contrast an analogy between the visual power of a Chinese character and that of his own language set in lines or groups of lines. The fusion of visual and verbal arts is not, however, the sole property of either Chinese or poetry, as any billboard in America will show. The art of designing inscriptions brought lines of language and nonrepresentational arrangements together long ago.

In drawing an analogy between the epigraphic and typographic arts, we must recognize the limitations of that analogy. Neither "Choral: The Pink Church" nor "The Desert Music" is particularly suitable for inscription on a wall or family vault. Still, because the history of English prosody has not prepared us to describe Williams's verse adequately, we need to look—for now—beyond its borders.

Sparrow differentiates between simple inscription (a date on a cornerstone, for example) and "literary" inscription. He defines the latter this way:

> A "literary" inscription, then, is a text composed with a view to its being presented in lines of different lengths, the lineation contributing to or enhancing the meaning, so that someone who does not see it, actually or in his mind's eye, but only hears it read aloud misses something of the intended effect. Such inscriptions are examples of a literary form that differs both from verse and from prose as it is ordinarily composed and presented.[27]

The presentation of a text "in lines of different lengths" recalls Tschichold's assertion that typography creates order out of "simple contrasting elements." The contributions that lineation and line division make to meaning are the subject of the previous chapter. The literary inscription, like many a poem by Williams, differs both from verse and prose "as it is ordinarily composed and presented." Prose is ordinarily printed in paragraphs whose lines are justified at both margins. Verse, by which Sparrow means metrical verse, is normally printed in lines "the length of which is determined by the metre," not the eye.[28] The literary inscription relies on lineation, spacing, and indentation to achieve its effects. It also relies, at least in the classical tradition, on the principle of symmetry. Here Williams differs. As we have seen, symmetry in the indented poems of *The Tempers* belongs to the realm of metrical verse as it is normally printed. Williams's more notable experiments in typography rely instead on a principle of asymmetry. They can be considered asymmetric inscriptions. We can see Williams choosing between these principles in the worksheets of "Choral: The Pink Church."[29]

First published in 1946, the poem suggests that "The Pink Church stands for the Christian Church."[30] The Church, however, is imagined at its inception, pink in the dawn light of Christianity, before Christ's teachings hardened into doctrines Williams saw as severe restrictions of the human spirit, especially among the New England Puritans. Both implicitly in the poem and explicitly in his comments on it, Williams draws an analogy between the original spirit of Christianity and the original meaning of communism.[31] Apparently this led some to interpret the Pink Church as the Pinko Church; yet Williams insists this is misreading. The Pink Church is not just the temple of Christ and Marx. It is also the temple of poetry, pink in the dawn of the imagination, the house from which song emanates:

> singing!
>     Covertly.
>        Subdued.                 [*CLP*, p. 159]

The song of the Pink Church is covert and subdued because its message is subversive. The Pink Church is the haven of the aberrant, the drunk, the prostitute, the fool, the mentally deranged, the suicide, the slaughtered, the famished, and the lonely. It is also the temple of the body, which Williams celebrates in the mode of the Song of Songs, praising the Church as a virgin with perfect breasts and pink nipples. This vision seems to owe much to Whitman, who is named once in the poem along with several others, but it is Milton who presides over the closing lines:

> Milton, the unrhymer,
>       singing among
>          the rest . . .
>
> like a Communist.                 [*CLP*, p. 162]

Milton, the unrhymer, sings covertly among the rhymers. The radical subversiveness of Christ, Marx, Whitman, and others finds its final expression in the image of Milton adopting a prosody of enjambment instead of rhyme, a prosody that produces verse for the eye, as Dr. Johnson said.

The prosody of "Choral: The Pink Church" is also subversive, promoting visual patterns beside auditory ones. The poem opens with a single tercet, its lines all left-justified. The lineation produces what can be considered three-stress lines, but the poem immediately subverts the stanzaic and accentual patterns, departing for irregular indentation, spacing, and margination. Several times along the way it considers triadic arrangements, as in the examples above, anticipating the appearance of the variable foot in *Paterson* two years later.

The tercet, however, is not the only form disrupted in the pink dawn of a new day; symmetry yields to asymmetry elsewhere, as in the sixth draft of the poem:[32]

> Proust's memory (in a cork
>         diving suit
> looking under the sea
>                     of silence)
> and bear witness:

———————————————

        —————————

——————————————

            —————————

———————————

The lines beneath the stanza are drawn in ink at the margin of this draft. They appear to mark an alternate line scheme. If adopted, this scheme would produce a symmetric arrangement: first and fourth lines left-justified, second and fifth lines indented farthest, third and sixth set in between. The six-line group falls into two triads. It is symmetric with respect to both horizontal and vertical axes. If Williams had opted in favor of symmetry, the final version of these lines might have looked like this (after he changed "and bear witness" to "to bear witness"):

> Proust's memory
>                     (in a cork
>         diving suit
> looking under the sea
>                     of silence)
>         to bear witness:

instead of this:

> Proust's memory (in a cork
>         diving suit
> looking under the sea·

                    of silence)
        to bear witness:                              [*CLP*, p. 160]

In designing his inscription, Williams rejects balance and symmetry. The asymmetric arrangement contrasts the longer left-justified lines with the short indented ones and the short indented ones with each other. The lines become dislocated as the call to the aberrant to come and bear witness takes its strange, parenthetical turn into a vision of Proustian memory as a diver exploring the depths of the unconscious. As it surfaces, the parenthetical material subverts the listing of names ("drunks, prostitutes, / Surrealists— / Gide and—"), throwing it temporarily off balance. The decision in favor of asymmetric inscription reflects the larger affirmation of all who have swerved from the straight and narrow way. Asymmetric inscription is itself something of an aberration in Williams's late poetry. Six years after "Choral: The Pink Church," symmetry became the norm and remained so for the rest of his life.


With his discovery of the variable foot Williams turned to symmetric inscription, a triadic stanza with its first line left-justified, second indented, third indented farther. Between 1952, when he published "The Orchestra" and an early version of the first twenty-four lines of "Asphodel, That Greeny Flower," and 1956, when "The Gift" and "The Turtle" were printed, Williams composed a total of twenty-eight poems in this format. A twenty-ninth, "The Descent," appeared in 1948 excerpted from *Paterson*, Book Two. According to Williams, this piece marks the birth of the triadic stanza, although, as noted, traces of it surface in "Choral: The Pink Church." On the other end, a fragment of the projected sixth part of *Paterson*, dated "7/1/61," shows the triadic arrangement, as does much of Book Five (1958). Although the stanza may have been coming and going for as many as fifteen years, Williams used it primarily during the years between the publications of the fourth and fifth books of his epic. Twenty-nine poems do not constitute a large part of Williams's complete work. Including *Poems* (1909), he wrote nearly as many sonnets. Still, Williams invested a great deal of time and energy explaining, celebrating, and promoting his discovery. As a result many of his readers have spent as much discussing it. The triadic stanza and its constituent, the variable foot, have become the proving ground for Williams's sense of prosody and our sense of that sense.

There are almost as many accounts of the triadic stanza as there are commentators. One of the more unusual comes from Hugh Kenner via Mike Weaver: "His eyes could follow a line but not jump back and locate accurately the beginning of the next line. . . . I'm convinced that the 3-ply typography of his late verse was originally a set of helps (with tab stops) for just such line-finding in rereading."[33] Weaver comments that, "although this suggests a physical reason why Williams increasingly used the 'triadic foot' in the last years of his life, the evidence of publication in *Paterson* in 1948 of 'The descent beckons' must be considered." Williams had his first heart attack in February 1948, the same month "The Descent" appeared in *Partisan Review.* His first stroke hit him in the spring of 1951. If we also consider the typography of "Choral: The Pink Church," Kenner's chronology seems shaky. Perhaps, having already experimented with the triadic stanza, Williams returned to it after his illness for the reasons Kenner states. Still, this would not explain why he abandoned the stanza for all but two of the poems in his last book. He did not get any healthier.

As Weaver implies, Kenner's account belongs to a critical tradition that includes Charles Olson's theory of "Projective Verse" and Oliver Wendell Holmes's "The Physiology of Versification" (1879).[34] Each of these represents what we might call a "physiological fallacy": the physiological organization of the body regulates the prosodic organization of verse. A line is a certain length because breathing takes a certain amount of time; accents recur regularly in a line because heartbeats recur regularly in the chest; lines are indented from the left margin because the eye has trouble moving to the left. Of course prosody can represent physiology, suggesting the rhythms of respiration, pulse, eating, speaking, or walking (as in "Sunday in the Park," *Paterson,* Book Two), but we cannot assign bodily functions a causal role in relations to prosody. If we did, how would we account for the range of prosodies throughout the history of the world? The lungs have always pumped, the heart has always beaten, but in some traditions we measure time, in others we count syllables, in others we mark accents. The range of verse forms grouped

under the heading "free" would alone be enough to suggest that no
two of us have bodies that work the same way.

Weaver's own account of the birth of the triadic stanza has much
to recommend it. He traces the arrangement to Pound's original
printing of "In a Station of the Metro":

> The apparition     of these faces          in the crowd:
> Petals          on a wet, black               bough.[35]

If these three-part lines were arranged according to the indentation
pattern of Williams's triadic stanza, they would look and read like
the poems of *The Desert Music* and *Journey to Love*. The problem with
Weaver's account is that chronology betrays him. Pound's poem was
printed in 1913, the year Williams published *The Tempers*. Are we
to assume that Pound's influence lay dormant in Williams's mind
for over thirty years, emerging suddenly in the second book of
*Paterson?* Surely the poems of the late teens and twenties would have
shown some mark of recognition, if Williams had been profoundly
struck by Pound's experiment. Perhaps the typography of *Kora in
Hell* is that mark. There is, however, no necessary link between the
original printing of Pound's poem and the inscriptional format of
the triadic stanza. Williams still had to come up with his own indentation scheme. The value of Weaver's account is that it recognizes
the importance of typography in the formation of Williams's stanza.
He does not succumb to either accentual or quantitative theories of
its format.

Those who do insist on such theories have Williams himself to
thank. His letter of May 1954 to Richard Eberhart is the most widely
recognized apologia for the variable foot.[36] After emphasizing the
necessity of "measure," by which he means "musical pace" (at least
here), and taking a shot at Whitman for writing verse with no discipline at all, Williams turns to analyzing two passages of his own,
one from "To Daphne and Virginia" and one from "To Eleanor and
Bill Monahan" (*PB*, pp. 75, 83). He numbers each of the lines of
his stanzas and then instructs Eberhart to "Count a single beat to
each numeral." Neither the word "time" nor "accent" appears in the
letter, although "beat" suggests a combination of the two. This letter
and its subsequent interpretations by Williams and others have led

to the isochronic theory of the variable foot. Charles Hartman summarizes the theory as follows:

> His [Williams's] own accounts approach those of Hopkins in obscurity. But evidence collected by Emma Kafalenos, in a dissertation called *Possibilities of Isochrony*, shows that Williams meant his three-line stanzas to be read so that each line occupies the same amount of time as the others. Lineation marks the isochronous units.[37]

Up to this point Hartman argues that an isochronic theory of free verse is inadequate. Why he should suddenly make an exception in Williams's case is unclear. The statement that "each line occupies the same amount of time as the others" raises many difficult questions. Consider these lines from "The Descent":

> The descent beckons
>         as the ascent beckoned.
>                 Memory is a kind
> of accomplishment,
>         a sort of renewal
>             even
> an initiation, since the spaces it opens are new places
>         inhabited by hordes
>                 heretofore unrealized ...   [*PB*, p. 73]

What can it possibly mean to say that the two lines "even / an initiation, since the spaces it opens are new places" occupy the same amount of time? Time on a stopwatch? A metronome? Reading time? Suppose a thousand people read the lines out loud a thousand times apiece. It is unlikely that one will be able to get seventeen syllables into the time it takes to say two, or draw out two into the time of seventeen, without distorting the words into something bearing little resemblance to the American idiom and its rhythms, rhythms the variable foot is supposedly built to carry. One could argue that to reason this way is to verge on the performative fallacy: Williams projected an abstract scheme, and whether or not anyone can perform it correctly is of no consequence. Still, an abstract scheme must include at least the possibility of being performed correctly. Perhaps

Williams intended for readers to pad shorter lines with musical rests. If so, what is the temporal standard by which they should measure the rests? One second? Two? The time it takes to read seventeen syllables? Perhaps "time" is not a matter of duration but a metaphor for attention and expectation. Then why all the talk of counting? Are readers supposed to pay as much attention to "even" as to "an initiation, since the spaces it opens are new places"? Perhaps in 1948 Williams had not yet refined his use of the triadic stanza. Consider instead "Asphodel, That Greeny Flower." In that poem appears a line of one syllable ("there") and a line of fourteen ("a voyage of discovery if ever there was one"). The problems remain the same.

Following Emma Kafalenos, Hartman tries to solve these difficulties: "The 'feet' vary in number of syllables and accents; but each occupies more or less the same amount of time as the rest. The reader is to adjust his pace according to the length of the 'foot.'"[38] Let us suppose we adjust our pace to read the word "even" slowly and then pause for a second afterwards—two seconds in all. Next let us suppose we move right along through the seventeen-syllable line—between three and four seconds. Compared to billions of years of geological history, one or two seconds is nothing; yet quantitatively the ratio is almost two to one. With that margin Homer's dactylic hexameter could have long syllables four times as long as the short, and a sonnet could have lines of twenty syllables. The point is that, if Kafalenos and Hartman are correct in saying Williams meant for each line to take "more or less the same time," it is no discovery at all. Most lines of poetry take more or less the same amount of time, if they have between two and seventeen syllables. Why then does Williams have so much to say about the variable foot as a prosodic innovation? Hartman argues that it is precisely because he has so much to say that the prosody is valid: "Williams became sufficiently well-known so that through letters and essays he could establish single-handedly the convention that all lines take the same time—though only for his own poems."[39] Because he said so, and people listened to him, it is true. This is doubtful reasoning.

Williams chose to make his stand on prosody and, within prosody, on the variable foot. His defenders attempt to unravel his letters and essays as though they were mystic texts,[40] while his detractors throw up their hands and pronounce him hopeless. The poems, however, remain. Why did he even bother with prosodic theory? The variable foot represents the culmination of Williams's private study. His reading took him through the pseudo-quantitative experiments of Campion; through Poe's "The Rationale of Verse" where the term "variable foot" is used to mean a metrical substitution which rescues a poem from tiresome regularity;[41] through Spanish poetry where he found the term *versos sueltos*, which means "blank verse" (Spanish poetry is "blank" if it has neither rhyme nor assonance), although he and his followers translate the term literally ("loose verses") and use it to signify the flexibility of the variable foot;[42] and through the essays and manifestos of Pound that return again and again to the need for a modern prosody based on musical cadence and quantity.[43] All his reading prepared him to discuss the auditory features of prosody. None of it prepared him to discuss the visual features of typographic inscription. When he discovered a typographic format that pleased him, he tried to explain it in terms derived from his reading. This borrowing of terminology from one prosody for another is hardly without precedent, as our habit of calling feet "long" and "short" shows. The prosody of the triadic stanza is a visual one. As with Sparrow's inscriptions, if you don't see it, you won't get it. The prosody depends on the visual conventions of nonmetrical lineation.[44] Enjambments and caesurae (another imperfectly borrowed term) disrupt line-syntax alignment, producing meaning in ways examined in chapter 1. Wagner's claim that "enjambment between feet is unnecessary because structure links the units into one line" needs reevaluation.[45] Without more radical enjambments to vary the phrasal sentence-diagramming, the triadic arrangement would soon become mechanical and tedious. To the conventions of lineation Williams adds indentation and symmetric stanza-patterning. Like metrical lines, this pattern is subject to substitution and variation: a single left-justified line will appear between two full triads, or a triad will have one line too few or too many (see "The Descent" for examples). Such variations do not imply a "variable stanza" analogous to a variable foot. Variations in stanza-patterning are defined against a fixed standard, whereas variable feet are not, because there is no fixed foot to vary against. These features of the triadic inscription did not burst forth suddenly in *Paterson*, Book Two. They evolved during the forty years following *Poems*

(1909), as Williams experimented with indentation patterns, verse paragraphing, and symmetrical and asymmetrical inscription.

Why did Williams choose a triad? Why not a dyad, tetrad, or pentad? Hartman defines a meter as "a prosody whose mode of organization is numerical."[46] According to this definition, the poems of *The Desert Music* and *Journey to Love* show a visual meter organized by the number three. Although Williams says to count beats, we are really counting lines. If there are any feet, or abstract units of periodicity in this meter, those feet are the stanzas themselves. But why three lines to a stanza? In attempting to construct a prosodic genealogy, we might look to Dante's *terza rima* and the symbolic association of its three lines with the Trinity, an association Williams himself implicitly acknowledges: "Dante was a craftsman of supreme skill, his emphasis upon a triple unity is an emphasis upon structure."[47] After appearing in poems by Shelley and Byron, *terza rima* descends into the twentieth century where the three-line stanzas of Stevens, though unrhymed, suggest a distant kinship. Among Williams's poems "The Yachts" stands out most clearly as an example of modified *terza rima*. Rhyme disappears after the first four lines sketch the interlocking *terza rima* scheme: *aba bxx*. Williams dangles the Dantesque pattern before us just long enough to make us wonder whether or not it is really there. Then, having hinted at prosodic ancestry, he abandons the model. The faint suggestion that "The Yachts" belongs to the powerful tradition of *terza rima* becomes troublesome when the poem swerves sharply into violence, forcing us to consider the poem as Williams's version of an Inferno set in the mind.

Although this diachronic account suggests possible sources of the triadic stanza, it does not answer the original question: Why use a triad at all? The poems of *The Desert Music* and *Journey to Love* do not invite the same kind of analysis as "The Yachts." We do not get very far asserting that Williams's triad symbolizes the Trinity. Apparently, however, the triadic structure did hold some kind of inherent appeal for him. Jerrald Ranta has shown that the principle of "tripartiteness" informs much of Williams's work.[48] According to Ranta, stanzas with three lines and poems with three stanzas or sections appear more frequently in *Collected Earlier Poems* than stanzas or poems organized by any other single number. Speaking of these poems, Williams admits that he was particularly fascinated by a few patterns, among them "the dividing of the little paragraphs in lines of three."[49] Many of his three-line stanzas represent quatrains he compressed and concentrated to make them "go faster." A cursory glance through *Collected Later Poems* suggests that the same may be true of that volume. Ranta does not suggest any reason for Williams's inclination towards triadic structures. Perhaps no single reason exists. Still, the phenomenology of tripartiteness provokes speculation. Where only two elements exist, we tend to see them in terms of binary opposition. With the addition of a third element, new structures emerge: beginning-middle-end, subject-middle-predicate, thesis-antithesis-synthesis.

A three-line haiku shows such a structure in its simplest lyric form. Usually the first line presents an image, the second extends or magnifies it, and the third abstracts it into metaphor, moral, or some larger meaning. If we consider its title as the first line, Pound's "In a Station of the Metro" is a good example. The haiku, however, is closed. The tripartite movement is completed within it. One of Williams's triads, on the other hand, does not always work so neatly. The end of the third line does not necessarily coincide with the closure of a three-part movement completely contained within the triad. In fact, such closed triads as these are rare:

> The ass brayed
>     the cattle lowed.
>         It was their nature.                    [*PB*, p. 62]

> Be patient that I address you in a poem,
>     there is no other
>         fit medium.                    [*PB*, p. 75]

> And I am not
>     a young man.
>         My love encumbers me.
>                                 [*PB*, p. 77]

> Love is that common tone
>     shall raise his fiery head
>         and sound his note.         [*PB*, p. 80]

It is all
        (since eat we must)
                made sacred by our common need.
                        [*PB*, p. 92]

There is nothing to eat,
        seek it where you will,
                but the body of the Lord.
                        [*PB*, p. 93]

By St. Francis
        the whole scene
                has changed.        [*PB*, p. 99]

They glimpse
        a surrounding sky
                and the whole countryside.
                        [*PB*, p. 99]

We will it so
        and so it is
                past all accident.        [*PB*, p. 126]

Happy the woman
        whose husband makes her
                the "King's whore."
                        [*PB*, p. 133]

What do I remember
        that was shaped
                as this thing is shaped?
                        [*PB*, p. 153]

Endless wealth,
        I thought,
                held out its arms to me.
                        [*PB*, p. 155]

Of asphodel, that greeny flower,
        I come, my sweet,
                to sing to you!        [*PB*, p. 161]

> The end
>           will come
>                     in its time.                    [*PB*, p. 165]

It is difficult to deduce a single three-part movement from these
examples. Sometimes the triad breaks syntactically after the first
line, sometimes after the second, sometimes after both, sometimes
not at all. We cannot say, for example, that these triads all tend
toward haiku-like structure, although one of them, the first, does.
What we can say is that lineation enforces a tripartite division of the
conceptual movement within each triad. Lineation gives each triad
its epigraphic quality. Even if there is no inherent three-part movement in thematic content, visual format makes each triad a three-
part inscription. Where we might not recognize tripartiteness if the
triads were printed as prose, we are now forced to see it. In choosing
the triad, Williams landscapes an utterance with a beginning, a middle, and an end. The symmetric format inscribes balanced parts
within the whole. If the stanza were dyadic, we would see antithesis
endlessly projected. If it were tetradic, we would see two sets of
pairs. If it were pentadic or larger, we would lose Dante's triple
unity to multiplicity.

If we take the triads above as standards of measurement, we can
use them as we used the one-sentence, noncaesural line in the last
chapter. Along with disjunctions between syntax and line boundaries, we can analyze the disjunctions between conceptual and stanzaic
ones, expanding the notion of enjambment to include all straddlings
of the divisions between triads. Part of the meaning of each poem
in *The Desert Music* and *Journey to Love* depends on these disjunctions,
their extent and character. In the opening lines of "The Ivy Crown,"
for example, we see alignment yield to disjunction:

> The whole process is a lie,
>           unless,
>                     crowned by excess,
>     it break forcefully,
>           one way or another,
>                     from its confinement—

or find a deeper well.
     Antony and Cleopatra
       were right;
they have shown
    the way. I love you
      or I do not live
at all.

Daffodil time
    is past. This is
      summer, summer!
the heart says,
    and not even the full of it.   *[PB*, p. 124]

Through the first three triads lineation corresponds to syntactic junctions within a sentence. Enjambments are relatively weak, because
they occur between phrases of that sentence, and the lines are uninterrupted by caesurae. As the "whole process" of love or life is a
lie unless it breaks from its confinement, so the whole process of the
verse is slack and monotonous unless it breaks predictable regularity
with variation. In the fourth triad it does exactly that, defying its
own regularity with a caesura in the second line and exceeding the
triadic limit with "at all," a typographic remainder which refuses to
be confined. As Williams proceeds with his meditation on confinement and excess, he wrinkles the verse surface with variations such
as these, small gestures of defiance that support a larger one:

     We are only mortal
but being mortal
    can defy our fate.   *[PB*, p. 124]

At the end of the poem, however, he smoothes the verse out with
a single self-enclosed triad, a typographic and conceptual configuration of wholeness and completion:

We will it so
    and so it is
      past all accident.

In addition to its variations, we need to consider one final aspect of the triadic stanza and its visual prosody: the indentation pattern. Having settled on symmetric tripartiteness, Williams could have chosen among many patterns for his inscription. He could have used the pattern sketched in the margin of the sixth draft of "Choral: The Pink Church." He could have placed the second line of the triad flush left, indenting the first and third. He could have opted for the mirror image of his stanza. One account of its visual format sees the triadic inscription as a piece of mimetic representation. When the format appears in the "Sunday in the Park" section of *Paterson*, Book Two, Paterson is walking around on top of Garrett Mountain. During the course of the afternoon, he goes up the mountain, witnesses the mysteries on top, and comes back down. The indentation pattern, the argument would go, mimes Paterson's descent. Rudolph Arnheim, following Heinrich Wölfflin, points out that because we read from left to right, we perceive any diagonal from upper left to lower right as descending, and from lower left to upper right as ascending.[50] The triadic inscription represents a series of downward steps, the steps Paterson takes as he returns from the mountain top, filled with the visions of the summit, Paterson, New Jersey's version of a modern Moses.

Thirty-five years earlier, at the Armory Show of 1913, Williams was particularly struck by Marcel Duchamp's "Nude Descending a Staircase," in which the figure is presented simultaneously at each stage of its descent. The descent motif informs Williams's work from *Kora in Hell* on, culminating in the gigantic image of the Great Passaic Falls.[51] Paterson's descent from Garrett Mountain parallels the descent of water over the falls. Any act of inscriptional mimesis that represents the former also represents the latter. These literal descents become, by means of the myth of Kora-Persephone, metaphorical vehicles for a figurative descent—into death, the past, the mind's hell, the profane—in preparation for a recuperative ascent. As Kora descends into Hades, we descend into the dead blankness of a world without art. When she returns in spring, imaginative vitality and beauty return with her. An invocation to Kora's return immediately precedes the passage Williams published separately as "The Descent":

> But Spring shall come and flowers will bloom
> and man must chatter of his doom     .     .

Paterson's descent, the Great Passaic Falls, Kora's voyage to the underworld, the descent of image and subject matter characteristic of Williams's verse—the triadic inscription mimes all these or appears to mime them in *Paterson*, Book Two, but what can we say of the other twenty-eight poems that use the same visual format? They do not each represent a waterfall or the descent from a mountain top. Are the poems of *The Desert Music* and *Journey to Love* all built on one huge prosodic allusion to *Paterson*, Book Two? Whenever we see the triadic stanza, are we to recall the complex of associations surrounding its "original" appearance? Williams did his best to promote this idea, claiming that the format and "The Descent" were born as twins. "Choral: The Pink Church" shows otherwise. Like the principle of tripartiteness, the descending indentation pattern has a prehistory in Williams's development. For one thing, in addition to the close of Whitman's "O Captain! My Captain," the pattern appears in the works of two other poets he read, Poe and Pound.[52] Although neither makes the systematic use of it that Williams does, both cut diagonally across the field of daisies now and then: Poe in "Tamerlane" and the 1843 version of "Lenore"; Pound frequently in the *Cantos*. Even without looking beyond Williams's own work, we find several examples. "The Wind Increases" and "Rain" both contain arrangements that cut from upper left to lower right in a step-like manner. Williams also uses a dyadic step pattern several times in his *Collected Earlier Poems*.

An important moment in the prehistory of the triadic stanza comes in "To Ford Madox Ford in Heaven," first published in 1940. Appropriately enough, Williams casts his poem in the dyadic typography of elegiac couplets. Although his lines are not metrical, their printing reflects the typographic convention of placing the hexameter flush left, while the pentameter is slightly indented. The regular alternation of longer left-justified lines with shorter indented ones proceeds smoothly until this variation:

> But, dear man, you have taken a major
>     part of it from us.
>         Provence that you
> praised so well will never be the same

Provence to us
        now you are gone.                           [*CLP*, p. 60]

The poem then returns to the elegiac pattern and continues without
variation to the end. Why should Williams vary the pattern here?
The added lines suggest the typographic analogue of hypermetrics.
Perhaps the reader is to infer that a sudden intensity of feeling forces
Williams beyond his measure. These lines do carry more pathos
than the rest of the poem, separating themselves from the ironic
flippancy that pervades it. Whatever the interpretation of this particular arrangement, its format leads to another account of the triadic
stanza, one that might complement the representation-of-descent
theory: the triadic stanza replaces the elegiac couplet, expanding the
typographic alternation of longer with shorter lines to distribute an
utterance more evenly. It is the modern elegiac format. The poems
of *The Desert Music* and *Journey to Love* may not talk of waterfalls and
mountain climbing, but each of them records the vision of an old
man who "must chatter of his doom." The poems of the middle
fifties constitute an elegiac meditation on death, time, and change.
In the inscriptional format of the triadic stanza, Williams finds a
visual design that is symmetrically elegant and dignified. Like the
elegiac couplet out of which it grows, the triadic stanza has many
uses, ranging from the celebration of erotic love to the lament for
mortality and the search for consolation. Reading each of the triadic
poems, we have the sense of an occasion, a ceremonial moment
inscribed on the page with a power and grace that certain works in
any age, even the modern, possess. Williams himself seems to have
sensed the inscriptional formality and expressive elegance of the
triadic format, but these qualities also troubled him. He later com-
mented that his triadic-stanza poems were too "overdone, artificial,
archaic—smacking of Spencer [*sic*] and his final Alexandrine."[53] In
his restless crusade to measure, to wage the war between freedom
and discipline in nonmetrical verse, Williams balks at his own configuration of discipline when it becomes, for him, the confining
design of artificial convention.

# CHAPTER THREE

# The World Is Not Iambic

We do not live in a sonnet world; we do not
live even in an iambic world; certainly not in a
world of iambic pentameters.

—"VS" (1948)

Exploring Williams's theory of measure entails a certain amount of deciphering, translating, and filling in of blanks. Here is what Williams says his verse is doing, and here is what it actually does. Can the two be reconciled? They can, but the reconciliation requires first solving some basic problems in Williams's terminology. The first two chapters have been concerned primarily with solving these problems, problems that have to do with formal schemes. Lineation, enjambment, caesurae, and typographic design all are matters of the surface patterning of verse. This chapter turns from a discussion of measure-as-scheme to the consideration of measure-as-trope. If Williams is using "measure" figuratively, what is it a figure of? Although several passages in his critical prose might provide starting points, I shall begin by looking to the Theatre of Trope, the poems themselves.

In "The Desert Music" (1951), a poem that combines autobiography with poetic creed, Williams considers measure at the outset:

How shall we get said what must be said?

Only the poem.

Only the counted poem, to an exact measure:
to imitate, not to copy nature, not
to copy nature

NOT, prostrate, to copy nature
                              but a dance! to dance
two and two with him—
                     sequestered there asleep,
                              right end up!
                                   [*PB*, pp. 108–09]

In the insistence on counting we hear the familiar rhetoric of formal
scheme. For him, Williams claims, getting said what must be said
necessarily involves poetry, and poetry necessarily involves verse
organized in some numerical mode, because no verse is free. But
although we may be tempted to take this statement at face value,
the verse scheme subverts that statement, establishing an early irony
in the poem. "The Desert Music" opens with a regular iambic pentameter line:

—the dánce begíns:     to énd abóut a fórm

If a "counted poem," that is, a metrical one, is the proper medium
for getting said what he must say, then all Williams has to do is
keep churning out stacks of iambic pentameter lines. But the counted
poem is not the proper medium, and the first few lines of "The
Desert Music" enact the rejection of a metrical scheme. In its quest
"to end about a form," meaning both a poetic form and the form
propped motionless on the International Bridge between Juárez and
El Paso, the poem begins by invoking and then departing from the
dominant scheme of its tradition. In its place "The Desert Music"
establishes the conventions of line-sentence counterpointing, which
are measured out against the standard of the one-sentence, noncaesural line "How shall we get said what must be said?"
Even though Williams's insistence on a countable scheme must
be approached cautiously, the phrase "an exact measure" does seem
to have a meaning that transcends the specific, technical features of
versification. Having asserted that getting said what must be said

involves the poem, and the poem involves "an exact measure," Williams establishes a metonymic relation between how the poem says what must be said and the idea of measuring. With the added qualification "to imitate, not to copy nature, not / to copy nature," the meaning of the metonymy emerges. How shall we get said what must be said? By means of measuring what we must say with imitation. Although formal scheme will inevitably figure in the mimetic project, it is only a part of that project. Many misreadings of Williams, as well as some of his own confusions, originate here, in the inference that he is saying reductively, the way to make poems that say something is to invent a nonmetrical formal scheme based on pseudo-quantitative theory.

In "The Desert Music," then, measure is a trope of mimesis, the poetic mode Williams deems most appropriate and effective for getting said what must be said; to imitate is to measure. Using "measure" this way, he taps the etymological meaning "to be meet," that is, commensurate, fitting, or appropriate. In the course of the poem, the embodiment of this mimetic measuring appears in the person of the "worn-out trouper from the states," a stripper dancing in a bar south of the border. The description of her gyrates through five neatly symmetric quatrains before yielding to the asymmetry of verse paragraphing, the typographic format Williams reserves for a shift in tone:

> What the hell
> are you grinning
> to yourself about? Not
> at *her*?
> The music!
> I like her. She fits
>
> the music                    [*PB*, p. 115]

The final typographic isolation of "the music" extricates this phrase from its immediate literal context and associates it with the figurative music of the desert. She fits, or measures, both the actual music she is dancing to, a striptease played "perfunc- / torily" by a "conventional orchestra," and an "insensate" music in the mind, an organizing aesthetic principle which the mind projects onto fragments of experience and perception. She is, for Williams, the emblem of mimesis. Stripped of covering fictions and illusions, the bored, exhausted dancer confronts us with the pathetic shabbiness of an imaginative desert; and yet "There is a fascination / seeing her shake" as "One is moved but not / at the dull show" (*PB*, p. 114). What is fascinating and moving about her is the "grace of / a certain candor" (*PB*, p. 115), which she retains by not pretending to be anything more or less than she is. In the same way, the poem gets said what must be said: that out of the barrenness of reality, "the dull show," comes the material to be shaped candidly into an aesthetic configuration.

The association of measurement with imitation in "The Desert Music" represents a single instance of a discussion that runs through letters, essays, and other poems. The authority to whom Williams refers throughout this discussion is Aristotle, particularly the Aristotle of the *Poetics*. As with other authorities he cites, however, the boundary between what comes from Aristotle and what comes from Williams's understanding of Aristotle is not always clear. While writing "The Desert Music," Williams told Kenneth Burke that recently he had come to understand the real "significance of Aristotle's use of the word 'imitation.'" He then moves to the formulation found in "The Desert Music":

> The imagination has to imitate nature, not to copy it—as the famous speech in *Hamlet* has led us to believe. There is a world of difference there. The whole dynamic of the art approach is involved, to imitate invokes the verb, to copy invokes nothing but imbecility. It is the very essence of the difference between realism and cubism with everything in favor of the latter.[1]

Whereas the distinction between imitating and copying may be implicit in Aristotle's *Poetics*, as Aristotle revises Plato's disparaging view that mimesis involves merely counterfeiting external appearances (*Republic*, Book Ten), Williams's formulation here owes more to Coleridge. In all imitation, Coleridge argues, two elements must coexist: likeness and unlikeness, or sameness and difference. In a genuine imitation there must be "likeness in the difference, difference in the likeness, and a reconcilement of both in one." If there is only likeness to nature "without any check of difference," then the would-be imitator has produced a mere copy, so that "the result is disgusting, and the more complete the delusion, the more loathsome the effect."[2] Returning to Williams's example of the difference between realism and cubism "with everything in favor of the latter," we infer that, for him, the superior mimetic power of cubism originates in its combination of a recognizable likeness to reality with a radical difference from it.

Although he claims to grasp the real significance of Aristotle's word "imitation," Williams does not, for example, wrestle out the implications for modern lyric poetry of a theory concerned primarily with tragic action or epic narrative. Although he might have, he does not locate in Aristotle's discussion of plots a sanction for his own conception of poetic structure. Instead, Williams's borrowings from Aristotle are selective. One aspect of the *Poetics* he apparently found attractive is its discussion of prosodic matters. Mariani states that in 1937 Williams suggested to Zukofsky that they collaborate on a book about modern prosody which would begin with Aristotle.[3] In the language and argument of this passage from the twenty-fourth chapter of the *Poetics* appear formulations Williams might have enlisted in his cause:

> As for the meter, the heroic measure has proved its fitness by the test of experience. If a narrative poem in any other meter or in many meters were now composed, it would be found incongruous. For of all measures the heroic is the stateliest and the most massive; and hence it most readily admits rare words and metaphors, which is another point in which the narrative form of imitation stands alone. On the other hand, the iambic and the trochaic tetrameter are stirring measures, the latter being akin to dancing, the former expressive of action. Still more absurd would it be to mix together different meters, as was done by Chaeremon. Hence no one has ever composed a poem on a great scale in any other than heroic verse. Nature herself, as we have said, teaches the choice of the proper measure.[4]

"Nature herself . . . teaches the choice of the proper measure." Lifted from its immediate context, this statement could easily serve as the slogan for several versions of mimetic or organic theory, as it confers on formal scheme—in this case, heroic measure—mimetic power. In rendering his translation of Aristotle, S. H. Butcher uses "measure" in two different ways. First, he uses it specifically in the phrase "heroic measure" (*hērōikon*) as a synonym for "meter," having used "meter" to translate the Greek *metron*. But, second, in the final sentence of the passage he chooses "proper measure" for *harmotton*, accusative form of a noun derived from the verb *harmozō*, which means "to fit well," "to suit," "to be adapted for," or "to be in tune." Williams read Butcher's translation, published in 1932, at the Gratwick farm in July 1949.[5] Butcher's double use of "measure" accurately reflects the basic Aristotelian notion that in a poetic imitation measurement takes place at two levels. Here Aristotle insists on a relation between these levels, asserting the fitness of a particular meter for epic poetry, which he calls "the narrative form of imitation." In arguing for this fitness, he links the prosodic measurement of verse scheme to the mimetic measurement of narrative poetry.

Although the linking of verse measurement to mimetic measurement might seem obvious to anyone, like Williams, who leans toward an organic theory of poetic form, Aristotle's assertion that Nature (*phusis*) teaches the choice of the proper measure can be misunderstood out of context. Construed one way, it could mean that there must be a natural, or organic, relation between verse measurement and mimetic measurement, the kind of relation, Williams argues, only nonmetrical verse can provide. But, as the rest of the passage shows, this is not at all what Aristotle has in mind. For him the "natural" relation of meter to matter is not organic, at least in any sense that American poets since Whitman would understand; it is highly conventional, with poetic conventions based on the fitness of a particular meter for a particular matter: heroic for epic narrative, iambic for action, trochaic for dancing. In the case of heroic meter, for example, its appropriateness for epic poetry rests not on anything inherently dactylic in the adventures of Odysseus, but on the ease with which dactylic meter accommodates the "rare words and metaphors" Homer uses to describe those adventures. There is, however, nothing inevitable or necessary about the relation of dactylic meter to the subjects of epic narrative; that relation arises from literary custom or usage, Aristotle's "test of experience."

This subtlety may have escaped Williams altogether, or he may have chosen to ignore it. At any rate, he does assume a necessary relation between verse measurement and mimetic measurement, as seen in the unfinished essay "Measure" (1959):

> What I in my American world am proposing is that they divide their lines differently and see what comes of it. We are finished with the aberration of free verse, but we have to learn to recount, taking our idiom as a constant (and for that we have to know what we are talking) and make units of it which we compose into our effects.[6]

The mimetic nature of lyric poetry differs from that of epic or dramatic, because the lyric poem does not imitate events or actions. Instead, it imitates speech, or "ahistorical utterance."[7] According to Williams, the speech of Americans constitutes an idiom that is distinct from British English. Therefore, Williams implies, lyric poems which purport to imitate American speech must break with the conventions of English prosody. In the passage above he recommends that American poets "divide their lines differently and see what comes of it." What Williams hopes will come of it is that American poets, in taking "our idiom as a constant," will make prosodic units ("variable feet") out of linguistic patterns and contours. Here Williams makes the mistake of confusing the object imitated (an American idiom) with the design of the mimetic medium (nonmetrical verse patterns), which—because an imitation is a trope of the object imitated—is a confusion of trope and scheme. In fact, what Williams gets when he divides his lines "differently" is enjambment, and the relation of enjambed verse to American speech is just as arbitrary and, by now, conventional as the relation of dactylic meter to the adventures of epic heroes. Certainly there is nothing inherently or necessarily enjambment-like in the way Americans express themselves with words.[8]

Although Williams may not do justice to the complexities of Aristotelian mimesis, he does appropriate the Aristotelian idiom in expanding his concept of measure to include the act of imitation itself. Outside Williams's critical prose, measure and measuring ap-

pear most often as figurations of mimesis in *Paterson*, which is not
surprising, for, like "The Desert Music," *Paterson* meditates exten-
sively on the nature of poetry and the poetic project. As in "The
Desert Music," this meditation accompanies a wide display of verse
schemes, giving those schemes a peculiar self-reflexive status. They
serve Williams not only as the media for his imitation, but also, in
moments when *Paterson* contemplates itself, as self-conscious examples of their own mimetic power. Beyond these immediate similarities to "The Desert Music," however, lie the unique features of
*Paterson* as a long poem in the American tradition that descends from
Whitman's "Song of Myself" and includes the long poems of Eliot,
Crane, Stevens, Pound, Zukofsky, and Olson. As a long poem,
*Paterson* must confront the problems of its own form, working to
create an imitation of the heterogeneous man-city, while also contending with its own formal heterogeneity. How can *Paterson* fashion
unity out of such diversity? This is its major theme.

In making both its mimetic and its prosodic measurements, the
long poem must avoid disintegrating into a sequence of fragments.
A showcase of verse forms, *Paterson* struggles continually with its
own fragmentation. Punctuated with prose interludes, the formal
surface of the poem is also fractured repeatedly by shifts among
various verse arrangements: long lines, short lines, verse paragraphs,
unrhymed couplets, tercets, quatrains, triadic stanzas, sapphics, and
short rhymed songs. Occasionally ghosts of an iambic pentameter
appear to recall a superseded order, as in "The province of the poem
is the world" or "What end but love, that stares death in the eye?"[9]
Operating throughout the poem are the conventions of line-sentence
counterpointing and typographic inscription, both symmetric and
asymmetric. Lines are fragmented, pages are fragmented, sections
are fragmented. Even the poem itself is a fragment, for, with a sixth
book projected, it remains unfinished. Against the threat of so much
disorder Williams's immediate defense is the three-part structure he
builds into each of the five books. Like the triadic stanza, the three-
part structure landscapes its material with a recognizable, predictable
measure. A numerical mode of organization, the three-part structure
provides each book and the poem as a whole with a controlling
"meter."

Williams's second defense against the threat of his long poem disintegrating into fragments—or rather, against the charge that it does so—is to explore the relation of verse measurement to mimetic measurement as a theme in the poem itself, implicitly arguing for the appropriateness of his form. To the end of Book One he appends a quotation from John Addington Symonds's *Studies of the Greek Poets* (1880):

> N.B. "In order apparently to bring the meter still more within the sphere of prose and common speech, Hipponax ended his iambics with a spondee or a trochee instead of an iambus, doing thus the utmost violence to the rhythmical structure. These deformed and mutilated verses were called [choliambi] (lame or limping iambics). They communicated a curious crustiness to the style. The choliambi are in poetry what the dwarf or cripple is in human nature. Here again, by their acceptance of this halting meter, the Greeks displayed their acute aesthetic sense of propriety, recognizing the harmony which subsists between crabbed verses and the distorted subjects with which they dealt—the vices and perversions of humanity—as well as their agreement with the snarling spirit of the satirist. Deformed verse was suited to deformed morality." [*P*, p. 53]

As with any of the other prose sections of *Paterson*, we wonder how to read this quotation. Is it indeed an explanatory note to take at face value? Or, as with many of Eliot's notes to *The Waste Land*, should we be on guard against irony and evasion? The safest answer is "Both." At the outset of *Paterson* Williams announces that his poem is "a reply to Greek and Latin with the bare hands," an attempt to fashion out of modern American life and speech a poem worthy of inclusion in an epic tradition. Against the background of this announcement, a direct invocation of classical models arouses suspicion that Williams is perhaps patronizing the university scholar and his love of Greek, Latin, libraries, and footnotes. At the same time, however, *Paterson* shows again and again that replying to the classical tradition involves bringing ancient forms into the modern poem in order to renovate them for use in the present, whether it be the stanza of Sappho, the idyll of Theocritus, or the dance of the satyr.

Given that Williams's quotation of Symonds should be approached with caution, the passage is a full and suggestive one. In the poetry of Hipponax Williams finds a model for doing the utmost violence to metrical structure in order to bring his measure into the sphere of prose and common speech. By suggesting an analogy between ancient poetic practice and his own project, Williams anticipates the objection that poetry which makes use of prose rhythms is in fact not poetry at all. Beyond this simple analogy, however, lies Williams's tacit acceptance of a theory of poetic form that sees in the relation of verse scheme to mimetic trope an underlying "harmony" and "propriety." A certain kind of verse is "suited to" a certain kind of subject matter.

Clearly, Aristotle's notion of the fitness of the proper measure hovers behind Symonds's terminology, as it does behind Williams's etymological sense of measurement as meting out, or allotment according to what is meet, fitting, or proper. But the passage from Symonds is more than a mandate for verse schemes that are mimetically appropriate. After all, many a passage from Aristotle could provide Williams with that. More important, in the context of *Paterson*, this passage points to a particular kind of verse and subject matter combined in the poetry of Hipponax. Symonds describes the lame or halting verses of Hipponax as being to poetry "what the dwarf or cripple is in human nature." When distorted subjects, such as the vices and perversions of humanity, are under scrutiny, mutilated, crabbed verses, which range freely into prose and common speech, are in order. That Williams took this truth to heart is clear from a letter he wrote John Holmes six years after the publication of Book One:

What shall we say more of the verse that is to be left behind by the age we live in if it does not have some of the marks the age has made upon us, its poets? The traumas of today, God knows, are plain enough upon our minds. Then how shall our poems escape? They should be horrible things, those poems. To the classic muse their bodies should appear to be covered with sores. They should be hunchbacked, limping. And yet our poems must show how we have struggled

with them to measure and control them. And we must SUC-
CEED even while we succumb.[10]

Williams's graphic language describes the poems of the modern age
as maimed, monstrous creations embodying terrible knowledge; and
yet, for all their monstrosity, these poems are meted out appropriately to the monstrous world they imitate. Hunchbacked, limping
verse suits a long poem about, among other things, the way men
and women behave and misbehave in an age marked by historical
trauma and psychological fragmentation; but the example of Hipponax, as Symonds interprets it, has other implications. Hunchbacked, limping verse also suits "the snarling spirit of the satirist,"
who employs derision, irony, and wit to expose and criticize the
deformed morality of our vices and perversions. As a poet Williams
is only sometimes a satirist, and as a satirist he is only sometimes a
snarling one. Still, his quotation of Symonds implies a recognition
that the fragmented body of *Paterson* suits not only its subject matter,
but also his own attitude toward the deformities of the man-city.

The always implicit and sometimes explicit argument of *Paterson*,
then, is that its verse schemes suit its imitation of the world. To
those who charge that the apparent fragmentation and overall formlessness of the poem render it a literary failure, Williams's answer,
I infer, would be that they have missed the point: the poem is
fragmented and apparently formless because it imitates the world,
and the world is often fragmented and apparently formless. In *A
Novelette* (1932), Williams comments on the fragmented technique
of *Kora in Hell*, defending its "shifting of category" against Pound's
anticipated criticisms. The shifting of category accounts, in Williams's view, for the "excellence" of his improvisations: "It is the
disjointing process" (*I*, p. 285). Setting aside the possible counter-
argument that an imitation of fragmentation and formlessness is not
necessarily rendered successful by being fragmented and formless,
we might take Williams at his word and read certain passages of
*Paterson* as further examples that measurement is simply a metaphor
for mimesis. These readings would find support in Williams's earnest
declaration that "not until I have made of it a replica / will my sins
be forgiven and my / disease cured" (*P*, p. 172). Here Williams as-
cribes to his poem not only the mimetic status of a literary work,

but also the supramimetic healing power of an icon or idol. Suddenly, the poetic act of imitation assumes a spiritual significance, which in turn may account for much of the missionary zeal behind Williams's crusade for the theory of measure.

The problem is that when Williams uses "measure" figuratively, it is not always as a simple figure of mimesis. Even though the mimetic meaning of measure is the one he recognizes and insists on, it is not always the meaning that particular passages and contexts point to. Furthermore, this same insistence sometimes leads him to make overly reductive statements about mimetic measurement, statements which interpret that measurement too narrowly, such as this one published in 1948, the same year as *Paterson*, Book Two:

> Look! the fixed overall quality of all poems of the past was a plainly understandable counting. The lines were measured and in general evenly arranged—to reveal a similar orderliness of thought and behavior in the general pattern of their day. Such measures (notice the word) were synonymous with a society, uniform, and made up of easily measurable integers, racial and philosophical.
>
> . . . Thus there was a correlation between the world as it stood politically and philosophically and the form of the poem that represented it—noticeably so in Dante's terza rima.
>
> . . . We do not live in a sonnet world; we do not live even in an iambic world; certainly not in a world of iambic pentameters.[11]

Whereas the assumption that "there was a correlation between the world as it stood politically and philosophically and the form of the poem that represented it" is reasonable enough, Williams overstates that correlative relation in order to challenge the assumption of Eliot's "Tradition and the Individual Talent" (1919). Rejected here is a recognition of the fundamentally conventional and traditional nature of verse schemes and poetic imitations. Certainly, a poet's attitude toward poetic form will reflect a larger attitude toward "an orderliness of thought and behavior," which in turn may even reflect a larger cultural ethos. As Williams argues in "Against the Weather" (1939), "Dante fastened upon his passion a whole hierarchy of formal beliefs . . . facing a time and place and enforcement which were his 'weather.' "[12] By casting his verse in *terza rima*, Dante revealed his attitude toward the theological and philosophical systems of his day: "The dogmatist in Dante chose a triple multiple for his poem, the craftsman skilfully followed orders—but the artist?"

But if poetic form reflects historical reality, the reality reflected is also that of literary history, not just political. The sonnet may have come into English poetic tradition at a particular moment, but that does not make it the sole property of that historical moment. The dogmatist in Williams, who seems to use polemical statements to jolt the reader out of intellectual complacency, wants to deny the historical continuity of culture in order to affirm its discontinuity, which, as Daniel Hoffman argues, "makes each moment, each act, each emotion experientially unique and therefore requires that style and form be provisional, experimental, reflective of the process of becoming self-aware rather than of the continuation of any familiar category of expression, thought, or feeling."[13] Once again Williams confronts us with a metonymy that collapses the series of complex links between a culture and its verse. By arguing that measures are "synonymous" with particular moments in social and political history, he not only reduces the mimetic function of those measures to a crude, historically determined mirroring; he also evades the meanings of measure which point back to him.


In making the verse measurements of formal scheme, the nonmetrical poem takes as its standard the verse line. In making the mimetic measurements of poetic trope, the imitative poem takes as its standard the spectrum of sameness and difference, or likeness and unlikeness, which Coleridge uses to distinguish an imitation from a copy. The relation between these two kinds of measurement must itself be measured by a standard of fitness, appropriateness, propriety, harmony, or suitability. Although Williams does not formulate his own poetics this way, his poems, letters, and essays show that these meanings all operate, at one time or another, behind the deceptively simple statement "Verse must be measured." In making the appeal to Aristotle, Williams's theory of measure secures these meanings; yet in securing them, Williams conceals another meaning of "measure" that Aristotle's theory of imitation does not allow.

Again in the twenty-fourth chapter of the *Poetics*, Aristotle states quite firmly, "The poet should speak as little as possible in his own person, for it is not this that makes him an imitator."[14] Implicit here is an assumption about the nature of poetry which the Romantic poets challenged and discarded. For them, for their nineteenth-century American counterparts, and for their modern heirs, the poet does not represent a transparent medium whose sole task is to imitate the external world; rather, the poet himself and his internal world are among the proper subjects of the poem. In turning to Aristotle's mimetic theory of poetry, Williams evades his own Romantic heritage, an expressive theory of poetry which authorizes the poet to speak in his own voice, and to speak often.[15] Here again, Williams's theory of measure appears to aim one way but in fact goes another. Even though he does not appear to value an expressive theory as highly as a mimetic one, his lyrics reveal a strong expressive impulse. In turn, this impulse confers on "measure" a second set of meanings, meanings that do not replace the mimetic ones, but hide behind them.

Like the mimetic, the expressive meanings of measure involve both verse scheme and poetic trope. As verse scheme, a given prosodic feature is mimetic if it imitates a phenomenon in the external world beyond the poetic structure; expressive if it signifies psychological or emotional activity in the internal world behind the poetic structure.[16] Thus, for example, the word-splitting enjambment Williams uses in "The Banner Bearer" is mimetic because it mimes the irregular gait of a limping dog. On the other hand, enjambments in "To a Poor Old Woman" are expressive because they serve as a series of prosodic signs for the psychological movement in the poet's mind toward stability and closure. Likewise, the typographic format of "Rain" (*CEP*, pp. 74–77) is mimetic because it mimes rain falling, and that of "The Pink Church" is expressive because its subtle creations of order correspond to mental operations of thought and feeling. In this context, the triadic stanza is particularly interesting, because at least once (in *Paterson*, Book Two) it seems to have mimetic value, whereas elsewhere it is purely expressive. Finally, the distinction between mimetic and expressive schemes expands an earlier formulation: when Williams counsels American poets to divide their lines differently in order to represent the American idiom accurately, he is insisting on the mimetic value of enjambment. In fact, however, Williams most often uses enjambment expressively. Those enjambments that are truly mimetic mime physical realities, such as a dog limping, rather than features of the spoken language.

In order for verse schemes to have expressive value, there must exist a link between those schemes and the mental worlds of the poet and the reader. It is in the recognition of this link that the Romantic theory of prosody originates, and with it another figurative meaning of measure for Williams. In his preface to the second edition of *Lyrical Ballads* (1800), Wordsworth defends the choice of metrical verse as his literary medium:

> The end of Poetry is to produce excitement in co-existence with an overbalance of pleasure; but, by the supposition, excitement is an unusual and irregular state of the mind; ideas and feelings do not, in that state, succeed each other in accustomed order. If the words, however, by which this excitement is produced be in themselves powerful, or the images and feelings have an undue proportion of pain connected with them, there is some danger that the excitement may be carried beyond its proper bounds. Now the co-presence of something regular, something to which the mind has been accustomed in various moods and in a less excited state, cannot but have great efficacy in tempering and restraining the passion by an intertexture of ordinary feeling, and of feeling not strictly and necessarily connected with the passion. This is unquestionably true; and hence, though the opinion will at first appear paradoxical, from the tendency of metre to divest language, in a certain degree, of its reality, and thus to throw a sort of half-consciousness of unsubstantial existence over the whole composition, there can be little doubt but that more pathetic situations and sentiments, that is, those which have a greater proportion of pain connected with them, may be endured in metrical composition, especially in rhyme, than in prose.

If poetry is the spontaneous overflow of powerful feelings, then meter is the premeditated regulation of powerful feeling by ordinary feeling. Wordsworth assumes a model of the mind that involves excitement, pleasure, and pain. In this psychic economy poetry produces excitement that should give pleasure, but which, under certain circumstances, may in fact give pain, either because the images and feelings it conjures are themselves painful or because the excitement produced exceeds its "proper bounds" and ceases to be pleasurable. The job of meter, then, is to reinforce these proper bounds by weaving into the fluctuations of powerful feelings a regular, familiar pattern of ordinary feelings. According to Wordsworth, meter serves a framing function, as it divests language of its everyday reality and throws "a sort of half-consciousness of unsubstantial existence over the whole composition." When we find ourselves confronted with too much excitement or pain in a poem, meter reminds us that, after all, this is just a poem, and its pain "may be endured." Particularly significant here are the equation of meter with feeling, albeit "ordinary," and the assumption that meter, "especially in rhyme," is not merely a literary convention, but also a psychological necessity. These are the marks of an expressive theory.

In his defense of meter Wordsworth concerns himself primarily with the psychological effects of metrical regularity. When he argues that the end of poetry is to produce pleasurable excitement, and that meter contributes toward this end, he adopts a reader's point of view. Reading *Lyrical Ballads*, we depend on meter to help us through our encounters with "the more pathetic situations and sentiments." In replying to Wordsworth several years later, Coleridge echoes some of his formulations but approaches meter from a different perspective:

> And, first, from the *origin* of metre. This I would trace to the balance in the mind effected by that spontaneous effort which strives to hold in check the workings of passion. It might be easily explained likewise in what manner this salutary antagonism is assisted by the very state which it counteracts; and how this balance of antagonists became organized into metre (in the usual acceptation of that term) by a supervening act of the will and judgement, consciously and for the foreseen purpose of pleasure. . . . There must be not only a partnership, but a union; an interpenetration of passion and of will, of *spontaneous* impulse and of voluntary purpose.

In the eighteenth chapter of the *Biographia Literaria*, Coleridge analyzes causes before effects and considers the originating mind of the poet before the receiving mind of the reader. The mental model implicit in Wordsworth's discussion becomes explicit in Coleridge's. Coleridge locates in the poet's mind a "salutary antagonism" of passion and will, "of spontaneous impulse and of voluntary purpose." For him meter is not merely a precautionary safeguard which the poet provides for his reader's psychological comfort; it is the full expression of one of two major principles in the mind, the principle of will and judgment which exerts itself "for the foreseen purpose of pleasure." Certainly, part of the pleasure foreseen will be the reader's, as later in the same chapter Coleridge compares the effects of meter to the effects of "a medicated atmosphere" or "wine during animated conversation," which "act powerfully, though themselves unnoticed"; yet another part of the pleasure will be the poet's, as he enjoys "the balance in the mind" which is achieved when "the workings of passion" are checked voluntarily. Coleridge makes clear that he differs from Wordsworth:

> The discussion on the powers of metre in the preface is highly ingenious and touches at all points on truth. But I cannot find any statement of its powers considered abstractly and separately. On the contrary, Mr. Wordsworth seems always to estimate metre by the powers which it exerts during (and, as I think, in *consequence of*) its combination with other elements of poetry.

Considered abstractly and separately, meter has the power to maintain a "balance of antagonists" in the poem, which in turn represents a comparable balance in the mind. This mental balance is not static or frozen. It is the result of an ongoing struggle in which the balance may be temporarily lost or discarded in order, perhaps, to be later regained. The expressive powers of verse schemes, both metrical and nonmetrical, invite figurative expansion as those schemes become tropes for an internal world. Several statements by Williams reveal that he found this to be true. In "Free Verse," for example, he describes the variable foot as "a term and a concept already accepted widely as a means of bringing the warring elements of freedom and discipline together." In the phrase "the warring elements of freedom and discipline" emerges Williams's version of the Coleridgean antagonism between passion and will. Here he examines the psychological significance of formal scheme from a poet's point of view. On another occasion, however, Williams sounds more Wordsworthian, as he speaks from a reader's point of view in a letter to Byron Vazakas (November 1944), describing the "unimaginable pleasure it would be to read or to hear lines that remain unpredictable," while those lines retain "a perfect order, a meter to reassure us."[17]

As what he believes to be the mimetic power of verse schemes leads Williams to use "measure" as a trope for the entire mimetic project, so the expressive powers of verse schemes lead him to use it as a trope for psychological conditions and necessities. These two figurative meanings are by no means mutually exclusive, as the mimetic and expressive qualities of formal schemes are not mutually exclusive. Thus, for example, Coleridge can maintain that poetry is one of the imitative arts even as he locates the origin of meter in the operations of the mind. Similarly, Symonds can argue that the limping iambics of Hipponax suit both the deformed morality of the men and women whose actions he imitates and the snarling spirit of the satirist himself. The mimetic and expressive meanings of measure-as-scheme and measure-as-trope do not exclude each other because they are both referential, with the mimetic referring to aspects of an external world and the expressive to those of an internal one. When in "The Wanderer" Williams asks, "How shall I be a mirror to this modernity," he is recognizing that in the modern poem the mimetic and the expressive inevitably complement each other. The problem is that in his own formulations Williams attends more often and more eagerly to mimetic meanings than to expressive ones. This is not so difficult to understand because, if one is going to argue publicly for a theory of verse that has larger implications for a theory of poetry, it makes more sense to dwell on meanings that reside in the public domain. It would not be particularly effective to argue that verse must be measured because I, William Carlos Williams, need measure; yet this would have been, in many ways, the truth.

The psychological significance of measure for Williams may account in part for the obsessive quality of his theorizing. Many poets have theorized and written about prosody, but few, if any, with the persistence of Williams, a persistence that sometimes borders on the monomaniacal. One could argue that his pioneering efforts required such theoretical support. But if this were true, we would be justified in expecting comparable theoretical support from other pioneers, such as Milton or Whitman; yet, aside from an introductory note on the verse or a paragraph in a preface, we do not find it. Even the statements of Hopkins, whose notion of sprung rhythm engendered explanations in several letters and a five-page "Author's Preface," do not match either the sheer quantity or the rhetorical fervor of Williams's. One crucial difference between Williams and Hopkins is that when Williams deliberates publicly on the prosody of poems, he also deliberates publicly on the prosody of the human self, on its organizing patterns, laws, and conventions. In the chapter on "Projective Verse" in the *Autobiography* he draws this analogy:

> Charles Sheeler, artist, has taken the one rare object remaining more or less intact (I omit the spacious wooden barn) a stone unit of real merit stylistically and proceeded to live in it—with Musya, a Russian of tragic past but vigorous integrities, and make a poem (a painting) of it; made it a cell, a seed of intelligent and feeling security. It is ourselves we organize in this way not against the past or for the future or even for survival but for integrity of understanding to insure persistence, to give the mind its stay.
>
> The poem (in Charles's case the painting) is the construction in understandable limits of his life.[18]

To give the mind its stay, to integrate our understanding, to construct understandable limits for our lives, to organize ourselves—for Williams this is what it means to make a poem, and what it means to measure.

The specific events and circumstances of Williams's life which may have contributed to the psychological significance of measure are beyond the boundaries of this discussion. Mike Weaver, Reed Whittemore, and Paul Mariani have all advanced the work of opening up Williams's life and mind for scrutiny, work that Williams himself began with his *Autobiography* over thirty years ago. His own concise summation of himself to Tom Cole (April 7, 1954) is sufficient to point us in the right direction: "My own work has had only one objective: to bring order out of chaos."[19] For Williams measurement involves bringing order out of chaos: formal schemes bring the order of verse out of the chaos of language; imitation brings the order of poetry out of the chaos of reality; and self-organization brings the order of discipline and will out of the chaos of freedom and passion. Revealed in Williams's statement to Cole is a perception of himself and his work that is radically dualistic. It suggests a private cosmology that pits a creative, ordering principle against an entropic, disordering one. In expanding into an expressive metaphor, "measure" comes to signify one side of this duality, the side Denise Levertov calls "Apollonian." In her essay "Williams and the Duende" Levertov distinguishes Williams's Apollonian "form-sense," which tends toward control, austerity, sobriety, and solemnity, from a Dionysian tendency, which "encompasses the dark, the painful, the fierce."[20] Here Levertov provides yet another set of terms to describe the divisions Williams recognized both within himself and between himself and the world. Ultimately, his theory of measure, with its inconsistencies and contradictions, leads us to contemplate an internal world in which to measure is to attempt what Coleridge would call "a balance of antagonisms," and what Williams, borrowing from Hyman Levy's *A Philosophy of Modern Man* (1938), calls "antagonistic cooperation" (*P*, p. 208). The poems express this attempt.

In *Paterson* the longest sustained meditation on measure appears in Book Two:

> Without invention nothing is well spaced,
> unless the mind change, unless
> the stars are new measured, according
> to their relative positions, the
> line will not change, the necessity
> will not matriculate: unless there is
> a new mind there cannot be a new
> line, the old will go on
> repeating itself with recurring
> deadliness: without invention
> nothing lies under the witch-hazel
> bush, the alder does not grow from among
> the hummocks margining the all

    but spent channel of the old swale,
    the small foot-prints
    of the mice under the overhanging
    tufts of the bunch-grass will not
    appear: without invention the line
    will never again take on its ancient
    divisions when the word, a supple word,
    lived in it, crumbled now to chalk.          [*P*, p. 65]

First published in 1948, these lines echo Williams's statement in the "Author's Introduction" to *The Wedge* that there is no poetry of distinction without formal invention. Under examination here is the triadic relation which exists among the stars, the mind, and the line, standing respectively for an external world, an internal one, and the poem itself. This passage is a dense one, packing into twenty-one lines a mythopoeic fable about order and creation. The word "measured," which appears here only once, invokes Einstein, whose measurements of the stars "according / to their relative positions" further revised twentieth-century cosmology, as Copernican measurements had revised that of Ptolemy. Furthermore, behind the reference to Einstein, whom Williams managed to cast as the champion of the variable foot, hovers a muted allusion to the original act of "invention" which spaced the stars in the heavens according to "the word, a supple word," or the Logos of Genesis. One could argue at this point that because Williams is saying that a change in the poetic line depends on a change in perception of the external universe, measurement here points toward mimesis, so that the poetic line must reflect the relative measurements of astrophysics. In fact, Williams has said as much on more than one occasion.

But our reading must reckon with a third party, the mind. A change in the poetic line also depends on a change in the mind which invents the line. In appropriating Einstein's notion of relativity, Williams borrows a metaphor for perception, a metaphor that authorizes his pursuit of the mind's fragmented flight from particular to particular in the disjunctive schemes of his verse. Those schemes, then, are not simply imitations of the relative measurements between stars; they are also expressions of the way perception works, as it generates the chaotic jumble of impressions which we must then attempt to order. In this context, measurement becomes Williams's term for the fundamental act of mind which brings order out of the chaos of perception. It, too, is an act of invention, as it brings to our conscious attention certain features of the external world, consigning others to oblivion.[21]

Without these acts of mental measurement specific details in a landscape would never be differentiated from one another and, at least for the inadequately attentive perceiver, would not exist: nothing would lie under the witch-hazel bush, the alder would not grow from among the hummocks, the small footprints of mice would not appear. In claiming this, Williams acknowledges—or confesses—the tendency of the poet's subjectivity to shape his imitation. Suddenly, the ontological status of the external world is challenged and, with it, the possibility of realizing what Aristotle meant by the word "imitation." As the boundary between external and internal worlds blurs, so does that between Aristotelian mimesis and modernist expressiveness. The difficult nature of these boundaries is the subject not only of this passage from *Paterson*, but also of the entire "Sunday in the Park" section, which opens "Outside / outside myself / there is a world" (*P*, p. 57). An external world may well exist outside the mind, but in some ways, according to Williams, its existence depends on the mind's inventive measurements of it.

The "Without invention" passage exemplifies the self-reflexive quality of verse schemes in *Paterson*. Like "The Desert Music" it begins with a line that invokes the old line, iambic pentameter:

Withóut invéntion nóthing ís well spáced

Having been invoked, however, the old meter is immediately deformed like the iambics of Hipponax, by, in this case, the halting, mutilating conventions of line-sentence counterpointing. These conventions enable Williams to frame specific features of language and landscape, thereby expressing the mental measurements of perception. Notable examples of this framing are the line "the small footprints of mice" and the self-descriptive enjambments "new / line" and "ancient / divisions." The line "the small foot-prints of mice" is the shortest of the passage, which might lead some to argue for its mimetic meaning: a short line, or "foot," suits small footprints; yet the line also has expressive value, as it aligns the most extreme variation in verse patterning with the most extreme variation in attention. The line corresponds to a moment when attention, which earlier had been devoted to the huge motions of the stars, comes suddenly and dramatically to rest on the smallest features of the landscape, the footprints of mice. As for the enjambments, they straddle not only line boundaries, but also the boundary between mimetic and expressive functions, because they point right to the poetic structure, rather than outside or behind it. The enjambment "a new / line" initiates a new line, also a short one, whereas "ancient / divisions" enacts a line division.

In the closing lines of the passage Williams alludes to the imagined origins of poetry, which elsewhere he envisions this way:

> Poetry began with measure, it began with the dance,
> whose divisions we have all but forgotten but are
> still known as measures. Measures they were and we
> still speak of their minuter elements as feet.[22]

The ancient divisions, then, are the divisions of the dance at the prehistoric, primal moment when poetry precipitated out of ancient ritual. In Williams's reconstruction of this scene, those ancient divisions conformed to an ordering principle, "the word, a supple word." In the final lines of "Without invention" he suggests that the new line, with its opposition to the sentence, allows him to recover the suppleness of these ancient divisions, a suppleness they lost when they hardened into metrical conventions estranged from their ritual origins.

*Paterson* explicitly engages the theme of measuring a second time at its close:

> The measure intervenes, to measure is all we know,
>
>     a choice among the measures   .  .
>
>         the measured dance
>
> "unless the scent of a rose
>     startle us anew"

Equally laughable
   is to assume to know nothing, a
     chess game
massively, "materially," compounded!

   Yo ho! ta ho!

We know nothing and can know nothing  .
   but

the dance, to dance to a measure
contrapuntally,
   Satyrically, the tragic foot.  [*P*, pp. 277–78]

Here again Williams opens a passage with a line that can be interpreted metrically:

The méasure íntervénes, to méasure is aĺl we knów

Except for an extra unstressed syllable between the fourth and fifth stresses, this line shows a family resemblance to the alexandrine, right down to the medial caesura after its sixth syllable. As for the sense of the line, this quickly spreads in several directions. Preceding it are three triadic stanzas in which Williams recalls his grandmother's declaration that "The past is for those that lived in the past. Cessa!" Then follows a fragmentary thought:

  —learning with age to sleep my life away:
 saying  .

Perhaps "The measure intervenes" is what Williams will say repeatedly as he sleeps his life away; or perhaps measure is what intervenes in that sleepy saying, either interfering with it or bringing it out from chaotic mumbling into ordered statement. On the other hand, the period after "saying" suggests the end of one thought and the beginning of another. If this is true, then the closing lines of *Paterson* constitute a coda in which Williams turns to the subject of measure as a way of bringing his poem to a formal close.

In asserting that "to measure is all we know," Williams repeats a formulation he makes in a letter to John Thirlwall (January 13, 1955), the same letter in which he traces the origin of poetry to the divisions of dance:

> The first thing you learn when you begin to learn anything about this earth is that you are eternally barred save for the report of your senses from knowing anything about it. Measure serves for us as the key: we can measure between objects; therefore, we know that they exist.[23]

Although Williams's epistemology is not academically rigorous, this passage reveals his interest in the relation of a perceiving subject to an object world. In admitting only the knowledge of his senses, at least here, Williams leans heavily toward empiricism; yet his particular brand of empiricism necessarily involves measurement: "we can measure between objects; therefore, we know they exist." Logically a puzzling sleight of hand, this formulation shows that, for Williams, measurements of the external world mediate between it and his own internal world. Measure serves him as "the key" to the world outside himself. Returning to the close of *Paterson*, we take "The measure intervenes" to mean that the acts of measurement we perform, whether in a poem or in astrophysics, intervene between us and the world outside us; that these acts provide us with our knowledge of that world; and that the measurements which intervene between us and the world comprise the Wordsworthian intertexture, the co-present layer of something regular, which reassures us in our transactions with that world.

That Williams is in fact confronting the dualism of our experience becomes clear with the lines " 'unless the scent of a rose / startle us anew.' " Here he quotes, or slightly misquotes, the final lines of his own poem "Shadows" (first published in 1955), a poem cast in triadic stanzas, which considers the two worlds we experience "violently" every day:

> two worlds
>           one of which we share with the
>           rose in bloom
>                     and one,

by far the greater,
             with the past,
                      the world of memory,
       the silly world of history,
             the world
                      of the imagination.        [*PB*, p. 151]

From these lines we see that Williams's statement to Thirlwall about
his empiricism needs qualification, because the empirically verifiable
world, the one shared with the rose in bloom, is surpassed in significance by the greater world inside the mind. In the final lines of
"Shadows" Williams acknowledges that the greater world of memory
and imagination "feeds upon" the object world of the rose. Alluding
to "Shadows" at the end of *Paterson*, Williams suggests that the
measurements which provide us with all we know of the object world
are not merely gratuitous; they are crucial because, without them,
we would be denied access to the world on which our imaginations
feed.

But measure does not intervene only between internal and external worlds; it also intervenes between two antagonistic sides of
an internal world. In the final image of the dance, "to a measure /
contrapuntally, / Satyrically, the tragic foot," Williams collects the
major themes of his poem. On one level, these lines return to the
passage from Symonds and the mimetic value of verse schemes. The
measured verse dancing of *Paterson* is "contrapuntal" because it coun-
terpoints lines and sentences. In turn, this counterpointing suits the
subject matter of the poem at the same time that it expresses the
spirit of the satirist, who is invoked by the pun on "Satyrically."
The "tragic foot" describes the verse foot which has been crippled
to suit the material under satiric observation. But on another level,
the "tragic foot" points to the dancing satyr himself, a figure who
appears throughout *Paterson*. Here the distinction between Dionysian and Apollonian impulses comes into play. An attendant of Dionysus, the half-man, half-goat embodies erotic revelry in *Paterson*.
Once again Williams returns to the mythic origins of poetry with
an allusion to the link between the satyr and tragedy, a link Aristotle
recognizes in the *Poetics* when he states that tragedy originated with
the authors of the Dithyramb, the Greek choric hymn which de-

scribes the adventures of Dionysus.[24] In conforming "to a measure," satyric, Dionysian energies are checked by the Apollonian limitations of form, which in turn signify restraints that will imposes on passion. At the Festival of Dionysus the celebration would have included the ritual purification of neophytes, a ceremony that finds its dramatic analogue in the purgation of passion, which, according to Aristotle, is the purpose of tragedy. As seen throughout *Paterson*, the tragedy of the modern satyr, whose passions are subject not so much to ritual purgation as they are to moral and social deformation, is that he is a severely limited version of his mythic prototype.

At the close of *Paterson* the intervention of measure expresses the "salutary antagonism" which Coleridge envisions, as one part of the mind exerts corrective pressure on another. That the effects of measurement are salutary, if not always ideal, is assumed by Williams. When he claims that in organizing the poem we organize ourselves "not against the past or for the future or even for survival but for integrity of understanding," he fails to recognize, or perhaps prefers not to recognize, that for him self-organization is a matter of survival, not merely an intellectual luxury. In some of Williams's statements on measure we detect an urgent tone which underscores his belief that health depends on the limitations of form, and on the Apollonian limitations that express: "[we need] some sort of measure, some sort of discipline *to free* [us] from the vagaries of mere chance and to teach us to rule ourselves again" (Letter to Thirlwall, June 13, 1955).[25] Even more explicitly, having announced in "On Measure—Statement for Cid Corman" (1954) that "Without measure we are lost," Williams goes on to discuss his own poetic experiments with the triadic stanza. Then he adds, "There will be other experiments but all will be directed toward the discovery of a new measure, I repeat, a new measure by which may be ordered our poems as well as our lives."[26] Here the salutary effects of verse measurement seem overstated, because prosodic order and psychological order are interchangeable only in a highly figurative, expressive sense. Assuming this qualification, however, we can return to the poem in which the drive toward health, survival, and self-organization informs the quest for measure, "The Desert Music."

Although the apparent goal of "The Desert Music" is to discover a measured form commensurate with what Aristotle meant by im-

itation, in fact its goal is to reaffirm poetic power in a moment of
personal crisis. This reaffirmation also had its challenging public
side: Williams wrote the poem to be read before a particular—and
not overly sympathetic—audience, the members of the Harvard Phi
Beta Kappa Society. Early on in the poem the reader discovers that
this imitator speaks "in his own person":

>                                   —to tell
>               what subsequently I saw and what heard
>
>                                   —to place myself (in
>           my nature) beside nature
>
>                               —to imitate
>           nature (for to copy nature would be a
>               shameful thing)
>
>                           I lay myself down:        [*PB*, p. 110]

The poem sets out, then, not only to imitate the external world of
"nature," but also to express an internal one, the world of "my
nature." In "The Desert Music" this self-expression centers around
dinner at a restaurant where Williams is meeting new people. Prior
to this scene the poem establishes a mood of anxiousness and self-
doubt with the question "Or / am I merely playing the poet?" (*PB*,
p. 116). Then, after several stanzas describing the restaurant, comes
the introduction of strangers:

>                           So this is William
>           Carlos Williams, the poet        .
>
>                           Floss and I had half consumed
>           our quartered hearts of lettuce before
>           we noticed the others hadn't touched theirs        .
>           You seem quite normal. Can you tell me? Why
>           does one want to write a poem?
>
>                       Because it's there to be written.

Oh. A matter of inspiration then?

Of necessity.

Oh. But what sets it off?                                    [*PB*, p. 117–18]

The challenging tone of "So this is William / Carlos Williams, the poet" pushes Williams toward self-explanation, which quickly shades into self-defense. Enjambment here expresses an uncomfortable self-consciousness, as it extracts Williams's first name from his literary name and label, "the poet." Line division images the estrangement of a man from his reputation, from the name he has made for himself in the world. In that estrangement he finds himself momentarily cut off from the external world of people who do not expect a poet to "seem quite normal"; yet he also finds himself cut off from himself and his own sense of poetic identity. The crisis of the moment, and of "The Desert Music," involves the question Williams poses in "The Wind Increases": "Good Christ what is / a poet—if any / exists?"

In exploring this question, Williams's clumsy interlocutor initiates a series of questions which reads like a stichomythic Socratic dialogue on the origin of poetry. What emerges from the exchange is a distinction between inspiration and necessity, with Williams arguing that the poet writes a poem out of an inner need. "But what sets it off," asks the reliable questioner. For an answer, however, he receives only this disconnected, typographically dislocated self-annunciation:

I am that he whose brains
are scattered
    aimlessly

The poet may seem quite normal, but inside disorder plagues him. With his brains "scattered / aimlessly," Williams is the plaything of "the vagaries of mere chance." Whether his mind is disordered because he is a creative thinker or because he is fighting his way back from his first stroke, Williams's great need, the need that sets off a poem, is to discover shape and order within the mind—to measure.

Only the poem provides this order, "Only the counted poem, to an exact measure." When Williams asks, "how shall we get said what must be said," he leaves his own question unexamined. By the end of "The Desert Music," however, we understand that what must be said is that William Carlos Williams is a poet because only the poem, with its formal schemes and figurative tropes, encloses a world that is sufficiently ordered. The music the stripper dances to, the central trope of the poem, is an image of measured order, pattern, structure, organization. At the end of the poem Williams's description of the music as amniotic fluid, which surrounds and protects us, reveals the hold it has on his imagination. A poet, then, is one whose creations can usher both him and us into a realm where we experience for a moment the shaped order of a self-enclosed, autonomous system. In making his final declaration, Williams uses enjambment to focus on the moment when the self realizes itself, its own separate identity and power:

> I *am* a poet! I
> am. I am. I am a poet, I reaffirmed, ashamed

> [*PB*, p. 120]

At the instant when the "I" discovers its verb waiting in the next line, the poet's creative power is revealed. Here the assertion recalls the Romantic reading of Exodus 3:14 ("And God said unto Moses, I AM THAT I AM"), on which Coleridge builds his definition of the primary imagination "as a repetition in the infinite mind of the eternal act of creation in the infinite I AM," and which Emerson invokes as the test of self and power in "Self-Reliance": "Few and mean as my gifts may be, I actually am, and do not need for my own assurance or the assurance of my fellows any secondary testimony." For Williams the progress toward reaffirmation of his primary imagination as a poet, and of his self-reliance as a man, begins in "The Desert Music" with the affirmation of an exact measure. In that affirmation he seeks a balance of antagonisms in the mind, a balance without which he would lose both creative power and self-reliance.

A few years later (1955), in a quieter mood, Williams considers measure and its implications in "Asphodel, That Greeny Flower." Throughout the poem an iambic presence gently reasserts itself:

Of ásphodél, that gréeny flówer,

I cóme, my sweét,

to síng to yóu!                    [*PB*, p. 161]

In "Asphodel" measure does not yield the small footprints of mice
or the suppleness of the ancient line; nor does it intervene because
it is all we know; nor does it authorize the proclamation of creative
power and self-reliance. Instead, what is most notable about measure
is its absence:

For there had been kindled
more minds
than that of the discoverers
and set dancing
to a measure,
a new measure!
Soon lost.
The measure itself
has been lost
and we suffer for it.
We come to our deaths
in silence.
The bomb speaks.                    [*PB*, pp. 167–68]

As Williams prophesies to Cid Corman, without measure we are
lost, and our lost condition, as a society and as individuals, occasions
Williams's appeal to his wife. We are lost amidst historical confusions, foremost among them the atomic bomb, which in "Asphodel"
expands into a figure for destructive forces no longer held in check.
In the face of historical confusion and the loss of social, political,
and moral restraints, Williams retreats into a personal world of memory, imagination, and confession. In that world the search for emotional order to compensate for the loss of other orders leads to the
simple affirmation of love against destruction, darkness, and death:

So let us love
confident as is the light

                    in its struggle with darkness
        that there is as much to say
                and more
                        for the one side
        and that not the darker
                which John Donne
                        for instance
        among many men
                presents to us.                    [*PB*, p. 180]

In a plea for love and forgiveness, Williams spiritualizes the
concept of measure with a meaning that extends beyond the technical
matters of poetic form. Exploring this meaning in the essay "Measure" (1959), he supplements the argument of "Asphodel" with another formulation:

> Measure, to be universally applicable, has to go into the
> provinces of abstract thought. To be practical that is, we have
> to know where a ballistic missile is going. Not approximately
> where it is going, but exactly where it is going. When your
> wifes [*sic*] goes out the back door you can't take a chance on
> it, you have to know where she is heading. Not approximately
> where, but exactly where she is heading in all its possibilities.
> When she returns at the end of the day you have only to look
> at her for an answer. That's what makes life interesting. That
> is why we are alive—love conquers all. That is the measure
> that dictates the structure of the lines of our poems.[27]

Beyond, or behind, the poem lie the provinces of abstract thought
into which the concept of measure continually takes Williams. The
word "abstract" appears to relate to a skill based on considerable
practice and both shrewd and loving attention. In inviting us to
follow him, he chooses the analogy of a ballistic missile, which, after
"Asphodel," we associate with darkness and destruction. Following
Williams's elliptical logic, we find ourselves comparing the measured
path of a missile with the path of a wife going out the back door.
The "measure" in question is the result of long familiarity, intimacy,
and experience. His point here is the same as that of "Asphodel":
against the disorders of social and political history, Williams has

ordered his life in and around a marriage, which is a kind of measure. With this expansive figuration, the meaning of measure dilates to answer "the riddle of a man and a woman," as Williams calls it in *Paterson*, Book Three. For him this riddle is in many ways the ultimate one, animating many mimetic and expressive arrangements alike. That in attempting to solve the riddle he should push his favorite concept to, and perhaps beyond, its limits as a trope, makes poetic and psychological sense. But then the sudden contraction of trope into scheme is confusing: "love conquers all. That is the measure that dictates the structure of the lines of our poems." Through this reductive rush from Supreme Fiction to verse practice flashes the urgent wish to make measure "universally applicable." In his crusading way Williams undertook to make measure nothing less than universally applicable to the human situations a poem addresses. In addition, he undertook to make it universally applicable to the tradition from which his poems come.

"Measure serves for us as the key." In context Williams means by this that the measurements we make between objects confirm their existence. Although as an epistemological proposition this statement vexes with its incompleteness, as a proposition about the aesthetic theory of William Carlos Williams it radiates a truth which its immediate context cannot contain. Measure serves Williams as the key to many of the questions poetry raises. As a prosodic term, it addresses the question, What is the nature of the modern verse scheme? As an aesthetic concept, it addresses the question, What is the nature of the modern mimetic project? As a richly expressive metaphor, it addresses the question, What are the psychological and emotional needs of modern men and women? As "measure" slides along a spectrum of meanings from scheme towards trope, denotation towards connotation, it allows Williams to examine the various relationships a poem maintains: poem to language, poem to world, poem to reader, poem to poet.

One relationship still remains to be examined: that of a poem to other poets, or poem to tradition. Of all the ways in which measure serves Williams as the key, this one has an importance that cannot be overestimated. For him measure serves as the key to the tradition, enabling him to confront the poets who, for various reasons, matter most. A full generation after Williams's death, his critics and admirers may argue that his poetry alone would have placed him squarely within the tradition, which may or may not be true. But, true or false, it is not the point; the point is that for Williams measure provided a sense of poetic mission. It gave him an ideological platform on which to build a campaign. Upon that platform measure secured itself a meaning which, no matter how much he preached and theorized, Williams could never exhaust.

Williams's theory of measure grew, in part, out of his response to Whitman. Poe's ideas of quantity provided Williams with theoretical sponsorship, which allowed him to circumvent Whitman, while claiming kinship with an earlier poet in his own tradition. But the theory of measure reflects Williams's confrontations with other poets as well. Twenty-two years after Eliot made his pronouncement on the subject, Williams took up the problem of tradition and the individual talent in a recently published essay, written in either late 1941 or early 1942, "Let Us Order Our World":

> He who will write the first ranking verse of his day will be he who expands the tradition to a point sufficient to bear the heaviest strains put upon it by the demands of the day without breaking down. That is, not only the style of the structural devices employed must be adequate to the strain they are expected to bear. New devices are necessary. You cannot fly through the clouds in a coach and four though the purpose remains the same, to arrive safely at the end of a journey: partly so, for there are today reaches of the understanding that were unattainable except to the imagination of former times.[28]

On the surface Williams's approach to tradition has little in common with Eliot's discussion of the shred of platinum analogous to a poet's mind, the escape from emotion, or the extinction of personality; yet this passage does reveal Williams's underlying commitment to what Eliot calls "the historical sense," rather than to the antihistorical discontinuity which surfaces in his remarks about Dante in "VS," published six or seven years later. Writing "first ranking verse" necessitates expanding the tradition, and typically Williams argues that, in order to expand the tradition, a poet must invent new "structural devices." Behind this phrase lies an allusion to, among other things, the new measurements of formal schemes. Shifting to an analogy of his own, Williams then turns to the inadequacy of a horse-drawn coach in circumstances that require an airplane. As usual, Williams masks his historical sense of literature with a metaphor which implies that poetry must make new discoveries and inventions the way science and technology have.

In the next paragraph the flying analogy reappears, but with a new perspective on expanding the tradition:

> Thus the complexity of modern thought, for one thing involving a complete change of base, often, as compared with former concepts, goes on increasing. And whereas all solutions are alike in beauty and simplicity when attained, the means to attain them will today involve enormous excursions of inventive skill before the answers can be brought home. Sometimes a man is flying upside down without knowing it and may be still advancing. Order is still there but you'd hardly recognize it for what it was formerly. Enterprises of the imagination must be made retroactive upon old rules which unless they permit limitless expansion cannot but be adjudged trivial or false. By release we confirm, by restraint we destroy.

An emphasis on "order" now joins the call for new structural devices. If Williams had written this essay ten or fifteen years later, he probably would have used the word "measure" instead. At any rate, we know we are on familiar ground because the notion of ordering leads directly to the dualities of limit and limitlessness, restraint and release. Here, however, Williams shrugs off the necessity of limits and restraint, calling instead for an "expanded, liberated, unrestrained tradition of verse."[29] A different tone appears four years after "Let Us Order Our World" when Williams, struggling with *Paterson*, writes in a letter to Kenneth Burke of awaking with "a half-sentence on my metaphorical lips, 'the limitations of form.' It seemed to mean something of importance."[30] This suggests that at other moments Williams did not find the limitations of form so easy to shrug off. That he should feel ambivalent towards those limitations comes as

no real surprise, however, for contradictions riddle his attitude toward the tradition from which he inherits them.

"Let us order our world." Perhaps revealing Williams's attitude
towards World War II, it is a catchy slogan, coming from a man
who enjoyed slogans in a period that generated many: the local is
the universal; no ideas but in things; verse must be measured. This
particular slogan is characteristic of Williams's thinking, which often
recalls an Elizabethan world picture, as it fuses the microcosmic
order of the poem to the macrocosmic orders of the world and
universe. "Let Us Order Our World" caps a period of four or five
years during which Williams turned repeatedly to the subject of
order in his essays, notably in "The Basis of Faith in Art" (1937?)
and "Against the Weather: A Study of the Artist" (1939). In the
former, for example, Williams stages an imaginary dialogue with his
brother, who accuses him of having a disorderly mind. Williams
answers:

> But you mentioned something about order—you said I had
> a disorderly mind. If to have a mind in which order is broken
> down to be redistributed, then you are right, not otherwise.
> . . . But order is in its vigor the process of ordering—a function
> of the imagination—[31]

Here Williams anticipates the self-description in "The Desert Music": "I am that he whose brains / are scattered / aimlessly." His
description of the imagination as the faculty which disorders so that
it can reorder recalls Coleridge's distinction between primary and
secondary imaginations. Soon after this statement, in the middle of
Williams's career, the concept of measure begins its dramatic expansion from prosody into mythology. This is no coincidence. In
calling for order in our poems, our lives, and our world, Williams
speaks out of his own beliefs and needs; yet in relying on the word
"order" again and again, he finds himself tangled in the slogans of
others. There was Stevens's invocation of order in *Ideas of Order*
(1936), particularly in "The Idea of Order at Key West": "Oh! Blessed
rage for order, pale Ramon, / the maker's rage to order words of the
sea." And, besides Stevens, there was Pound, whose ideas of order
may have drained the term of its usefulness for Williams.

In Pound's Canto 13, published in the *Transatlantic Review* (1924) and in his *Draft of 16 Cantos* printed in 1925, appears this passage:

> And Kung said, and wrote on the bo leaves:
> > If a man have not order within him
> He can not spread order about him;
> And if a man have not order within him
> His family will not act with due order;
> > And if the prince have not order within him
> He can not put order in his dominions.
> And Kung gave the words "order"
> and "brotherly deference"
> And said nothing of the "life after death."[32]

In this passage Pound presents a Confucian idea of order: the social order depends on and reflects the ethical and spiritual order of society's leaders and citizens. This order finds itself expressed here in verse which combines the rhetorical rhythm of Confucian aphorism with a loose triple meter; through these techniques also surface traces of Whitman, as anaphora and syntactic parallelism lend the passage the smooth elegance and balance Whitman discovered in Biblical wisdom literature. As it stands, the argument of Canto 13 seems consonant with Williams's own thinking about the relation between psychological and social order. Nevertheless, in his essay "Excerpts from a Critical Sketch: *A Draft of XXX Cantos* by Ezra Pound" (1931), Williams reveals a crucial difference between himself and Pound:

> It is in the minutiae—in the minute organization of the words and their relationships in a composition that the seriousness and value of a work of writing exist—*not* in the sentiments, ideas, schemes portrayed.[33]

Implicit in the phrase "the seriousness and value of a work of writing" is a reply to Pound's essay "The Serious Artist," published in *The Egoist* in 1913, in which Pound argues that good art is art which "bears true witness," art which is most precise in its definitions of "the inner nature and conditions of man." Pound goes on to associate good writing with "perfect control" and "orderliness." Although one can easily overstate the importance of any one passage or, by singling out one cause, oversimplify a series of complex developments, Williams's reply to Pound prophesies the split between the two poets with uncanny precision. His own poetry is hardly without sentiments and ideas, but throughout his career Williams doggedly insisted on the primacy of "minutiae," on the "minute organization of the words and their relationships in a composition," whereas Pound led his *Cantos* deeper and deeper into "the sentiments, ideas, schemes portrayed." By 1935, when he published *Jefferson and/or Mussolini*, Pound's idea of order carried implications Williams found troubling: "The great man is filled with a very different passion, the will toward *order*."[34] The will toward order in the formal schemes of verse is one thing, but Williams felt in the fascism of Mussolini quite another.

Although Pound's ideas of order, both prosodic and social, unquestionably influenced Williams's own thinking about measure, it became imperative, for poetic and political reasons, that Williams establish some distance between himself and those ideas. The result was a new emphasis on "measure," which suddenly had to do double duty as a term for prosodic "minutiae" and as a conceptual basket for Williams's meditations on other aspects of the will toward order. The theory and mythology of measure, then, took shape in response to, among others, Pound. Pound is not the only poet Williams answers with measure, but more than other contemporaries Pound stood in Williams's mind for the crossing of poetic theory with social and political thought, a crossing that the theory of measure acknowledges but reexamines. Many of Williams's statements about measure have social and political implications, some of which he overstates for dramatic effect, but those implications do not eclipse his aesthetic concerns. This difference between Williams and Pound is the hidden subject of the "Without invention" passage in *Paterson*, the rhetorical structure of which suggests a reply to Pound's Canto 45:

> With usura hath no man a house of good stone
> each block cut smooth and well fitting
> that design might cover their face,
> with usura
> hath no man a painted paradise on his church wall
> *harpes et luz . . .*

> with usura the line grows thick
> with usura is no clear demarcation
> and no man can find site for his dwelling.
> Stonecutter is kept from his stone
> weaver is kept from his loom . . .
>
> Usura slayeth the child in the womb
> It stayeth the young man's courting
> It hath brought palsey to bed, lyeth
> between the young bride and her bridegroom .
>                    CONTRA NATURAM

Although Pound may appear to be adopting the manner of a medieval or renaissance preacher here,[35] anaphora, parallelism, and cataloguing once again suggest the influence of Whitman, to whom Pound had reconciled himself in "A Pact" (1913), requesting, "Let there be commerce between us." As the "commerce" between Pound and Whitman—the economic metaphor is telling—appears in the rhetorical schemes of Canto 45, so does the commerce between Williams and Pound appear in the rhetorical schemes of "Without invention." The similarities in surface patterning, however, only intensify the differences in thought, differences that begin with Williams's substitution of the antithetical construction "Without invention" for Pound's "With usura." Whereas Pound concentrates on the negative implications of an economic presence, Williams addresses the negative implications of an aesthetic absence. Pound's poem places men and women in the midst of economic, social, and historical forces. Williams's answer replaces images of men and women with images of stars, witch-hazel, alder, and mice, and it replaces economic, social, and historical forces with psychological and expressive ones. Pound's rhetoric realizes itself through tropes of production, Williams's through tropes of perception. These contrasts reflect the larger difference between Pound's conception of order and Williams's conception of measure, a difference also reflected here by the two treatments of "the line." When Pound declares "with usura the line grows thick," it is not obvious that he means the verse line, if indeed he does. Instead, the line grown thick serves as an image of the breakdown of "clear demarcation" between what is natural and what is, in Pound's view, a sin against nature. On the other hand, by the time Williams urges that "without invention the line / will never again take on its ancient / divisions," it is clear that he means the verse line and, with it, the minutiae of formal scheme. This is not to say that Williams no longer shares Pound's concern with economic and social orders; *Paterson* demonstrates repeatedly that he does. Rather, the differences between these two passages suggest that, for Williams, the path toward order, the ultimate order of "the word, a supple word," leads through the formal surface of his art.

If in Williams's mind Pound stood for the crossing of poetic theory with social and political thought, then Eliot stood for the limits and restraints of tradition. The theory of measure is as much an answer to Eliot as it is to Pound, but with this difference: while it widened the gap between Pound and Williams, despite an early closeness, the expansion of the term "measure" closed the gap between Eliot and Williams, despite a professed distance. Williams's unilateral campaign against *The Waste Land* and its author often discourages or distracts us from making important connections between the two poets; yet the vehemence of Williams's attack amounts to too much protesting, as though he found himself, much to his discomfort and annoyance, closely connected with Eliot in several ways. The point is not to assign either poet the role of originator and the other of imitator, but rather to identify features of Williams's theory of measure that seem to answer Eliot. Despite his immense learning and magisterial indifference to Williams, Eliot, too, has his limitations as a theoretician. Neither Eliot nor any of his critics has defined or adequately explained, for example, the difference between emotion and feeling ("Tradition and the Individual Talent"), an objective correlative ("Hamlet and His Problems"), or all the meanings of "music" ("The Music of Poetry"). Each of these terms poses interpretive problems, just as Williams's use of measure does. For this discussion, however, we need only remember that each poet interested himself deeply in the problems of modern verse schemes; that each poet was aware of the other; and that the two poets shared more than either cared to admit.

About the time Williams composed "Let Us Order Our World," Eliot delivered and published his lecture "The Music of Poetry"

(1942). Mariani asserts that when Williams read it, he became convinced that Eliot was stealing from him.[36] Whatever the merit of Williams's belief, he encountered "The Music of Poetry" at the crucial period when measure was expanding from term to theory. Many of the formulations he found in Eliot's lecture, whether they were indeed his or merely reflected his thinking, must have accelerated Williams's progress toward a theoretical platform of his own. Several times, for example, Eliot acknowledges "the law that poetry must not stray too far from the everyday language which we use and hear"; he echoes one of Williams's favorite formulations in speaking of the task of exploring "the relation of the idiom of verse to that of speech." When Eliot asserts, "The music of poetry, then, must be a music latent in the common speech of its time," he gives "music" a figurative meaning which Williams enlarges in "The Desert Music." When Eliot argues that "no poet can write a poem of amplitude unless he is a master of the prosaic," he gestures back to *The Waste Land* and confirms Williams's own discoveries. When Eliot traces the development of Shakespeare's style "from artificiality to simplicity, from stiffness to suppleness," he endorses the same quality Williams values in a supple word. But finally, and most important, when Eliot claims that "no verse is free for the man who wants to do a good job," he touches one of Williams's nerves.[37]

In "The Music of Poetry" Eliot notes that he had expressed his view on free verse twenty-five years earlier, an allusion to "Reflections on *Vers Libre*," published in 1917, the same year as Williams's essay "America, Whitman, and the Art of Poetry." In 1917 both poets agreed that good verse is never wholly free, but their subsequent arguments differ. Eliot's conclusion is that "There is no escape from metre; there is only mastery." He arrives at this conclusion, having made these assertions:

> But the most interesting verse which has yet been written in our language has been done either by taking a very simple form, like the iambic pentameter, and constantly withdrawing from it, or taking no form at all, and constantly approximating to a very simple one. It is this contrast between fixity and flux, this unperceived evasion of monotony, which is the very life of verse. . . .

We may therefore formulate as follows: the ghost of some simple metre should lurk behind the arras in even the "freest" verse; to advance menacingly as we doze, and withdraw as we rouse. Or, freedom is only truly freedom when it appears against the background of an artificial limitation.[38]

In 1917 Williams could not offer a theoretical alternative either to free verse or Eliot's arguments. Instead, his reply to Eliot unfolds during the next forty years in his theory of measure. In Eliot's terse formulations, Williams found himself confronted with two propositions, one of which he wanted to reject and the other to absorb. "Reflections on *Vers Libre*" pressured him to shape a response not only to Eliot but also to the tradition for which, in Williams's mind, Eliot stood.

The proposition which Williams could never bring himself to accept is that there is no escape from meter. Eliot's metrical ghost lurking behind the arras is, Williams argues, the phantom we can afford to be haunted by no longer, particularly the ghost of iambic pentameter: "We do not live in a sonnet world; we do not live even in an iambic world; certainly not a world of iambic pentameters." While this statement assumes a questionable relation between the historical world and poetic convention, it also carries with it another meaning. For Williams iambic pentameter amounts to much more than an old-fashioned verse scheme which does not easily accommodate the American idiom; it also stands for the entire tradition of English poetry from Chaucer to Tennyson. More than than, Williams associates iambic pentameter with the twentieth-century representative of that tradition, T. S. Eliot. His repeated denials of the pentameter, echoing Pound, mask his anti-Eliot polemic. In turn, this polemic is one of the major pressures shaping the theory of measure. The fiction of a "variable foot" allows Williams to have it both ways, as he appears to escape from meter and Eliot, while maintaining the necessary "contrast between fixity and flux," which Eliot—or before him Poe in "The Rationale of Verse"—considers the very life of verse. Williams's theory of measure then is, as well as an answer to Whitman and Pound, a theoretical apparatus designed to support a public response to Eliot.

The world is not iambic, the psyche is not iambic, the heartbeat is not iambic, breathing is not iambic, but the tradition is iambic. There is no escape from this truth, and Williams knew it, even in 1917 when in "America, Whitman, and the Art of Poetry" he seems to speak directly to Eliot: "But if by 'too much freedom' they mean that a man binds himself by ignoring truths he cannot escape, no matter how hard he may run, then I will listen." Williams did listen, and he heard, too. One of the great ironies of his career is that more than many of his contemporaries and self-proclaimed heirs Williams mastered meter, which, according to Eliot in "Reflections on *Vers Libre*," means mastering the "constant evasion and recognition of regularity." Enjambment, asymmetric typography, excursions into prose, the use of the vernacular, his own theoretical statements—all these are strategies to evade an iambic norm; and yet time and time again, as in "Seafarer," "The Wind Increases," "Good Night," *Paterson*, "The Desert Music," and "Asphodel," he recognizes that norm, allowing it "to advance menacingly as we doze, and withdraw as we rouse." When one thinks of modern masters of the iambic meter, one thinks of Yeats, Eliot, Frost, Stevens, and Crane. But the very fact that Williams does not appear on such a list—that he would not want to—confirms the success of his evasion. Unlike these others, Williams grounds himself not in metricality but in non-metricality. Against this background moments of iambic regularity become significant variations. As with many successful evasions, however, the most important act of concealment involves truth we conceal from ourselves. This is another crucial aspect of the theory of measure: the higher Williams piled letters, notes, essays, and poems preaching the escape from meter, the deeper he buried the truth in his own mind.

If Eliot's proposition that there is no escape from meter is one Williams wanted to deny, then this is the proposition he wanted to absorb and master: "Or, freedom is only truly freedom when it appears against the background of an artificial limitation." The theory of measure is predicated on this belief; Williams's fifty-year search for measure is a search for limitation, the ground against which his figures of freedom can appear. In "Let Us Order Our World" he claims to seek "limitless expansion" and release from restraints which destroy; yet in his essay "Free Verse" (significantly, he lists "Reflections on *Vers Libre*" in the short bibliography following the essay), he locates the origin of measure in the war between freedom and discipline. This opposition would seem to point toward Eliot's "Reflections on *Vers Libre*"; yet beyond Eliot stands the American prophet of limitation, Emerson.

In various ways Poe, Whitman, Pound, and Eliot all contributed, either directly or indirectly, to the multiple meanings of measure. Williams acknowledges each of these poets, mentions them frequently, and holds their images before him as he assembles his thoughts on the nature of verse. But Williams mentions Emerson rarely. In the *Selected Letters*, for example, his name appears once in a letter to Thirlwall (June 13, 1955), and even then he is mentioned only in passing:

> The history of American prosody shows itself to have been troubled by a concern for something wrong with our acceptance of verse forms handed down to us. Emerson was another in that sequence. Poe was another American poet who was made uneasy by the structure of verses and wrote an essay about its mathematical implications. Most were content to imitate their betters, the asses, and as a consequence wrote slavishly.[39]

Throughout his writings Williams remains strangely quiet about Emerson, who does not seem to be either a major contributor to the theory of measure or someone Williams seeks to challenge with that theory. He is merely "another in that sequence." Presumably, Emerson's statement in "The Poet" that "it is not meters, but a meter-making argument that makes a poem" would be welcome as another formulation in favor of a new measure, but Williams does not pounce on this passage and subject it to any sustained examination. One might be tempted, therefore, to grant Emerson a certain minimal importance as an earlier American poet, and then to dismiss him. Mariani, for example, discusses Williams's affiliation with the Unitarian church and the tradition that shaped Emerson. Later, he also alludes to Williams's "Emersonian bias";[40] yet, except for a few other isolated references, this is all we hear. The problem, however, is that while Emerson himself may seem to have little to do with Williams's theory of measure, Emersonianism has everything to do with it.[41] At the core of Williams's search for measure lies the American pragmatic effort to reconcile freedom with limitation.

In tracing the shadow of Emersonianism, we might recall a passage from *Spring and All*:

> The inevitable flux of the seeing eye toward measuring itself by the world it inhabits can only result in himself crushing humiliation unless the individual raise to some approximate co-extension with the universe. This is possible by aid of the imagination. [*I*, p. 105]

Emerson's name does not appear in *Spring and All*, but Emersonianism stamps this passage. In the arrangement of the seeing eye, the individual, the world or universe, and the imagination, emerges a distinctly Emersonian configuration. Through the agency of the seeing eye, or visionary faculty, the individual self realizes the antithetical relation which exists between itself and the world or universe (Emerson's Nature, or Not Me). This realization begets in the self a drive to defend itself against the power of the universe to crush and humiliate it. According to Williams, this defense "is possible by aid of the imagination." Whereas Emerson might have said "Reason" instead of "imagination," he makes the link between them clear in "Nature": "The Imagination may be defined to be the use which the Reason makes of the material world." In the Emersonian economy of *Spring and All*, measurements "can only result in" a confrontation between the freedom of the individual and limitations the universe imposes on that freedom. The challenge to the individual, then, is to rise "to some approximate co-extension with the universe," or, as Emerson would say, to discover power in self-reliance.

The Emersonian quality of Williams's thinking here is not limited to an apparent coincidence of attitudes; it also registers a striking rhetorical resonance. In 1866, for example, Emerson notes in his journal:

> But I am always struck with the fact that mind delights in measuring itself thus with matter,—with history. A thought, any thought, pressed, followed, opened, dwarfs nature, custom, and all but itself.[42]

As in the passage from *Spring and All*, measurement does not merely imply comparison with a standard; rather, it signifies a competitive struggle between the mind and matter, the former measuring itself and its freedom against the latter. This competitive, combative meaning of measure also surfaces in the essay "Fate," Emerson's most sustained meditation on freedom and its limits:

> History is the action and reaction of these two,—Nature and Thought; two boys pushing each other on the curbstone of the pavement. Everything is pusher or pushed; and matter and mind are in perpetual tilt and balance, so. Whilst the man is weak, the earth takes up him. He plants his brain and affections. By and by he will take up the earth, and have his gardens and vineyards in the beautiful order and productiveness of his thought. Every solid in the universe is ready to become fluid on the approach of the mind, and the power to flux it is the measure of the mind.

Emerson's assertion that the power "to flux" matter is the measure of the mind prefigures Williams's notion of the "inevitable flux" of the seeing eye toward measuring itself by the world. In the Emersonian arena, the freedom of flux, or fluidity, contends with the limitation of solidity. There is no easy coexistence possible between them, only constant struggle. When the mind measures itself against matter, it necessarily enters that struggle.

This Emersonian meaning of measure also informs Williams's theory of verse schemes, as well it might, because the life of verse depends on the contrast between fixity and flux. When Williams describes freedom and discipline, his name for limitation, as "warring elements," he states what is at stake for him in a poem. As the patterns of verse combine fixity and flux, limitation and freedom, they dramatize the larger Emersonian contest between mind and matter, or between the imagination and the world. As verse measurement assigns dominant power to fixity or flux in a particular poem, by grounding it in metricality or nonmetricality, it becomes, as Emerson would say, a measure of the mind. Now, if this is so, we might wonder why Williams would insist that there be discipline, fixity, or limitation in verse, when he is so outspoken a champion of freedom. Wouldn't it be more fitting to dispense with these altogether? The simplest answer to this is Eliot's: freedom cannot be recognized unless it appears against a background of artificial limitation. The regulation between freedom and limitation, he implies, is binary. Thus, for example, we might argue that without at least the implication of a fixed norm, a variation cannot appear as a gesture of freedom. Without an assumed norm, the argument would go, the poem presents nothing but confusion and apparent randomness, which is not the same as freedom. But, although this argument has a certain obvious truth to it, it fails to explain Williams's particular attitude toward limitation, an attitude that is essentially Emersonian.

In "Fate" Emerson is not concerned with artificial limitations; he is preoccupied with real ones:

> We cannot trifle with this reality, this cropping-out in our planted gardens of the core of the world. No picture of life can have any veracity that does not admit the odious facts. A man's power is hooped in by a necessity which, by many experiments, he touches on every side until he learns its arc.
>
> The element running through entire nature, which we popularly call Fate, is known to us as limitation. Whatever limits us we call Fate.

Several years after "Self-Reliance," his rhapsodic hymn to freedom, Emerson finds himself admitting the odious facts of fate. These he traces "in matter, mind, and morals; in race, in retardations of strata, and in thought and character as well." The point of Emerson's argument, however, is to convince us that "limitation is power," that quickly "fate slides into freedom and freedom into fate," and that it is "the best use of Fate to teach a fatal courage." Finally, with an interesting choice of words, Emerson returns to the relation between limits and measurements:

> We can afford to allow the limitation, if we know it is the meter of the growing man. We stand against Fate, as children stand up against the wall in their father's house and notch their height from year to year. But when the boy grows to man, and is master of the house, he pulls down that wall and builds a new and bigger. 'Tis only a question of time.

Here Emerson's word for measurement is "meter," the term that shuttles between the world of measurements and numbers and the world of verse. As meter is limitation in verse, limitation is meter in life. We can afford to allow this meter in the poems of our lives, as long as we realize that it measures our growth and does not suppress it.

For Williams measure carries, in addition to its other meanings, the connotations of Emersonian fate, the meter of our lives by which we know we have grown. When Williams concedes that a man may bind himself by ignoring truths he cannot escape, he acknowledges the presence of limitations, real not artificial. Several years after "America, Whitman, and the Art of Poetry," the older Williams, like the older Emerson, has to admit the odious fact of real limitations. The enlargement of measure into a private philosophy accompanies this admission. The theory of measure, with its many overlapping layers and twisting ramifications, represents Williams's attempt to teach himself a fatal courage, a courage that pervades, for example, "The Ivy Crown": "We are only mortal / but being mortal / can defy our fate." Limitation is power, in verse and in life, and measure is limitation. When Williams declares that without measure we are lost, he erases distinctions between the artificial limitations of prosodic convention and the real limitations of human existence. To measure is all Williams knows, and, in saying so at the end of *Paterson*, he answers Keats, the poet he first admired: not beauty or truth, but measure. Measure is all we know on earth, and all we need to know.

The last poem in which the word "measure" appears offers a parable about freedom, limitation, and poetry:

HEEL & TOE TO THE END

Gagarin says, in ecstasy,
he could have
gone on forever

he floated
ate and sang
and when he emerged from that

one hundred eight minutes off
the surface of
the earth he was smiling

Then he returned
to take his place
among the rest of us

from all that division and
subtraction a measure
toe and heel

heel and toe he felt
as if he had
been dancing                                    [*PB*, p. 69]

Published in July of 1961, "Heel & Toe to the End" celebrates the
flight of Yuri Alekseyevitch Gagarin, Soviet cosmonaut and first
man to orbit the earth in space. Once again, Williams finds in the
advances of science and technology a metaphor for poetry and the
poet. Gagarin also represents the explorer-discoverer, the hero of
Williams's imagination and a twentieth-century version of Colum-
bus. Here, however, exploration and discovery have not yielded the
new world of North America, but a new world of space, the Ein-
steinian realm where all measurements are relative. In addition to
these familiar figurations, Williams uses familiar schemes: nonmetrical verse ruled by enjambment, by variations in line lengths, and
by the tripartite format of three-line stanzas; and yet, against the
background of nonmetricality shimmers the iambic mirage:

Then he returned

to táke his pláce

amóng the rést of ús

As suddenly as it appears, the metrical phantom dissolves into
a meditation on measure, but its significance remains. "Heel & Toe
to the End" falls into two halves: the first describes Gagarin's flight
and ecstasy; the second, marked by the capitalized "Then," considers

his return to "his place among the rest of us." After the ecstatic voyage up and out, during which the lone self floats, sings, and wants to go on forever, comes the return to the place of the self among other selves. The verse becomes iambic as the freedom of Gagarin's discovery slides back into the fate of his ordinary life. But nothing in the poem suggests that the descent into limitation represents defeat. Instead, the poem moves from limitation to measure. As in *Paterson* or "The Desert Music," measure returns us to counting ("all that division and / subtraction") and to the foot, the ancient division of dance. In his ecstasy the explorer felt "as if he had / been dancing," as if his excitement found release, not restraint, in the regularity of aesthetic organization. The chiasmus "toe and heel // heel and toe" not only mimes the dance of the weightless cosmonaut; it also traces the chiastic pattern of restraint sliding into release, release into restraint. In his search for measure Williams traced this pattern many times; he watched it dance through his poems, heel and toe, to the end, as he sought to fashion out of the warring elements of freedom and discipline a principle to organize his poems and his experience. That a poem, like a life, must pattern itself in new ways when older ones fail is the discovery he made in his explorations of himself and his world. It is a discovery he brought back each time he returned to take his place among the rest of us.

# Notes

## INTRODUCTION

1 This essay was discovered by Mike Weaver among the papers of Viola Baxter Jordan. It appears in Weaver's *William Carlos Williams: The American Background* (Cambridge: Cambridge University Press, 1971), pp. 82–83.

2 *Letters of Wallace Stevens*, ed. Holly Stevens (New York: Alfred A. Knopf, 1966), pp. 407, 438.

3 Paul Mariani, *William Carlos Williams: A New World Naked* (New York: McGraw-Hill, 1981), p. 719.

4 John Hollander, *Rhyme's Reason: A Guide to English Verse* (New Haven: Yale University Press, 1981), p. 1.

5 William Carlos Williams [WCW as author in subsequent notes], "Measure," *Spectrum* 3, no. 3 (Fall 1959): 155.

6 A. Kingsley Weatherhead, "William Carlos Williams' Prose, Form, and Measure," *English Literary History* 33 (March 1966): 121.

7 Williams's belief in a time-based prosody does not seem to have been shaken by the argument against time and timers which took shape in 1959 with the assertion by William K. Wimsatt, Jr., and Monroe C. Beardsley that "Quantity is a dimension where you cannot make mistakes in pronouncing English"; the fact that the measurable features of verse occur in temporal succession, as in music, does not mean that the measurement of verse must be based on time ["The Concept of

Meter: An Exercise in Abstraction," *PMLA* 74 (December 1959): 589]. Since the publication of "The Concept of Meter," John Hollander and Charles Hartman have strengthened the argument, the former tracing the quantitative fallacy to poet-composers and Elizabethan prosodists [*Vision and Resonance: Two Senses of Poetic Form* (New York: Oxford University Press, 1975), pp. 3–90], and the latter exploring its twentieth-century versions in *Free Verse: An Essay on Prosody* (Princeton: Princeton University Press, 1980), pp. 32–44]. Those interested in the historical and theoretical background are referred to these discussions.

8   Weatherhead, p. 119.

9   Eleanor Berry, "Williams' Development of a New Prosodic Form— Not the 'Variable Foot,' But the 'Sight-Stanza,' " *William Carlos Williams Review* 7, no. 2 (Fall 1981): 21–30; Marjorie Perloff, " 'To Give a Design': Williams and the Visualization of Poetry," in *William Carlos Williams: Man and Poet*, ed. Carroll F. Terrell (Orono, Maine: National Poetry Foundation at the University of Maine, 1983), pp. 159–86; Henry Sayre, *The Visual Text of William Carlos Williams* (Urbana and Chicago: University of Illinois Press, 1983). Subsequent references to these works appear in the text.

10   Elsewhere I have argued that Sayre's approach to Williams's visual text is restrictively synchronic. Although he excels at recognizing patterns on the page as abstractions of order, he neglects or misses historical, diachronic legacies which surface in the shapes of Williams's poems. See my review in *Sagetrieb: A Journal Dedicated to Poets in the Pound-H.D.-Williams Tradition* 3, no. 2 (Fall 1984): 157–64.

11   *The Autobiography of William Carlos Williams* (New York: Random House, 1951), p. 51.

12   Stephen Tapscott, *American Beauty: William Carlos Williams and the Modernist Whitman* (New York: Columbia University Press, 1984), p. 14.

13   Tapscott, pp. 14, 16.

14   For example, Tapscott argues: "In effect, the triadic line itself is an extended dactyl, a single line composed of three 'variable' feet (each containing one to four syllables and one or two distinct stresses)" (p. 117). First, calling the triadic line "an extended dactyl" implies that in any given triad the first line is more prominent than the next two. The poems of *The Desert Music* and *Journey to Love* do not support this argument, nor do they show that each triad is made of three lines containing one to four syllables apiece. Second, Tapscott associates the tripartiteness of the triadic line with triple meters, such as the triple meter of "In Brueghel's great picture, The Kermess" (p. 117). Williams's triadic line poems rarely, if ever, approximate the metrical scheme of this or other triple meter poems.

15   WCW, "America, Whitman, and the Art of Poetry," *The Poetry Journal* 8, no. 1 (November 1917): 28, 29.

16   T. S. Eliot, "Reflections on *Vers Libre*," *New Statesman* (March 3, 1917).

17  WCW, "America, Whitman, and the Art of Poetry," p. 32.

18  *The Selected Letters of William Carlos Williams*, ed. John C. Thirlwall (New York: McDowell, Obolensky, 1957), pp. 135–36.

19  WCW, "An Approach to the Poem," *English Institute Essays, 1947* (New York: Columbia University Press, 1948), p. 66.

20  WCW, "An Essay on *Leaves of Grass*," *"Leaves of Grass" One Hundred Years After*, ed. Milton Hindus (Stanford: Stanford University Press, 1955), p. 22.

21  Walt Whitman, *Prose Works 1892*, ed. Floyd Stovall (New York: New York University Press, 1964), II, 440.

22  WCW, "An Essay on *Leaves of Grass*," p. 23.

23  Linda Welshimer Wagner, ed. *Interviews with William Carlos Williams: "Speaking Straight Ahead"* (New York: New Directions, 1976), p. 102.

24  WCW, *Selected Letters*, p. 287.

25  Alex Preminger, Frank J. Warnke, O. B. Hardison, Jr., eds., *Princeton Encyclopedia of Poetry and Poetics*, enlarged ed. (Princeton: Princeton University Press, 1974), p. 288.

26  WCW, "Free Verse," TS, Collection of American Literature, Beinecke Library, Yale University, New Haven, Connecticut.

27  *The Complete Stories and Poems of Edgar Allan Poe*, ed. Arthur Hobson Quinn and Edward H. O'Neill (New York: Alfred A. Knopf, 1967), II, 993–94. Mary Ellen Solt points to this essay in "William Carlos Williams: Idiom and Structure," *Massachusetts Review* 3 (Winter, 1962): 305; and in "William Carlos Williams: Poems in the American Idiom," *Folio* 25, no. 1 (1960): 4. Williams knew Poe's essay, along with several other of Poe's "firm statements on the character of form," which led Williams to announce that in Poe "American literature is anchored, in him, on solid ground" [*In the American Grain* (New York: New Directions, 1956), pp. 219, 226]. The judgment that American literature is anchored in Poe allows Williams to bypass Whitman in his retrospective search for a predecessor to sponsor his prosodic theory. Poe upholds a music-based, time-keeping theory of versification. Having begun "The Rationale of Verse" with the discussion of Uniformity and Variety— a discussion that culminates in his coining the term "variable foot"— he turns to the stuff of which verse is made: "What we start from in the very beginning of all idea[s] on the topic of verse, is quantity, *length*" (p. 1006).

28  Emily Mitchell Wallace, "The Satyrs' Abstract and Brief Chronicle of Our Time," *William Carlos Williams Review* 9, nos. 1–2 (Fall 1983): 140.

29  WCW, "America, Whitman, and the Art of Poetry," p. 33.

30  WCW, "Studiously Unprepared: Notes for Various Talks and Readings: 1940–1941," Collection of American Literature, Beinecke, Yale University, No. 4, n.p. These notes have been edited by Paul Mariani and published in *Sulfur* (1982): 12–13.

31  WCW, "Studiously Unprepared."

32  WCW, "Dartmouth College Talk," C49, Lockwood Memorial Poetry
    Collection, State University of New York at Buffalo. I am grateful to
    Robert J. Bertholf, curator, for his suggestion that this is a draft of the
    second Dartmouth speech (1945), not the first (ca. 1939), as listed by
    Neil Baldwin and Steven L. Meyers in *The Manuscripts and Letters of
    William Carlos Williams in the Poetry Collection of the Lockwood Memorial
    Library, State University of New York at Buffalo: A Descriptive Catalogue*
    (Boston: G. K. Hall, 1978).


CHAPTER ONE


1   WCW, *Imaginations*, ed. Webster Schott (New York: New Directions,
    1970), pp. 123–24. All subsequent references to this edition will appear
    in the text as *I*. I have benefited from Marjorie Perloff's discussion of
    this poem in *The Poetics of Indeterminacy: Rimbaud to Cage* (Princeton:
    Princeton University Press, 1981), pp. 125–29.
2   Hollander, *Vision and Resonance*, p. 235.
3   Mariani, p. 545.
4   *Princeton Encyclopedia of Poetry and Poetics*, p. 289.
5   Hollander, *Vision and Resonance*, p. 110.
6   Samuel Johnson, "Milton," *Lives of the English Poets*; quoted by Hol-
    lander, *Vision and Resonance*, p. 91.
7   WCW, *Autobiography*, p. 60.
8   WCW, [Philip and Oradie], Collection of American Literature, Bei-
    necke Library, Yale University, New Haven, Connecticut; this passage
    from the manuscript page appears in *Massachusetts Review* 3, no. 2 (Win-
    ter 1962): 307.
9   WCW, *Autobiography*, p. 60.
10  *The Collected Earlier Poems of William Carlos Williams* (Norfolk, Con-
    necticut: New Directions, 1951), p. 3. All subsequent references to
    this edition will appear in the text as *CEP*.
11  Hartman, p. 25.
12  For one example in the early poetry see "The Cod Head," *CEP*, p. 333.
13  *The Collected Later Poems of William Carlos Williams*, rev. ed. (Norfolk,
    Connecticut: New Directions, 1963), pp. 69, 92, 112, 114, 133, 145.
    All subsequent references to this edition will appear in the text as *CLP*.
14  E. E. Cummings, *Complete Poems 1913–1962* (New York: Harcourt Brace
    Jovanovich, 1972), p. 740.
15  WCW, *Paterson* (Norfolk, Connecticut: New Directions, 1963), p. 261.
    All subsequent references to this edition will appear in the text as *P*.
16  *Complete Poems of Marianne Moore* (New York: Viking, 1981), pp. 32–
    33.
17  WCW, *Pictures from Brueghel: Collected Poems 1950–1962* (New York:

New Directions, 1962), p. 5. All subsequent references to this edition will appear in the text as *PB*.

18  George Saintsbury, *Historical Manual of English Prosody* (London: Macmillan, 1910), p. 279.

19  Harai Golomb, *Enjambment in Poetry: Language and Verse in Interaction* (Tel Aviv: The Porter Institute for Poetics and Semiotics, Tel Aviv University, 1979), p. 41.

20  John Hollander, "The Metrical Emblem," *Essays on the Language of Literature*, ed. Seymour Chatman and Samuel R. Levin (Boston: Houghton Mifflin, 1967), p. 119.

21  Roger Fowler, " 'Prose Rhythm' and Metre," *Essays on Style and Language*, ed. Roger Fowler (London: Routledge and Kegan Paul, 1966), p. 88.

22  Samuel R. Levin, "The Conventions of Poetry," *Literary Style: A Symposium*, ed. Seymour Chatman (London and New York: Oxford University Press, 1971), p. 83.

23  Hollander, *Vision and Resonance*, p. 99.

24  WCW, *Autobiography*, p. 276.

25  Paul Fussell, Jr., *Poetic Meter and Poetic Form*, rev. ed. (New York: Random House, 1979), p. 88.

26  Justus George Lawler, *Celestial Pantomime: Poetic Structures of Transcendence* (New Haven: Yale University Press, 1979), p. 74.

27  Lawler, p. 42.

28  Leonard Meyer, *Music, the Arts, and Ideas* (Chicago: University of Chicago Press, 1967), pp. 10–11; partially quoted by Lawler, p. 13.

29  Leonard Meyer, *Emotion and Meaning in Music* (Chicago: University of Chicago Press, 1956), p. 31; quoted by Lawler, p. 42.

30  *The Caedmon Treasury of Modern Poets Reading* (New York: Caedmon Publishers, 1957).

31  Robert Frost, "The Figure a Poem Makes," *Complete Poems of Robert Frost* (New York: Holt, Rinehart and Winston, 1967), p. v.

32  Wimsatt and Beardsley, "The Concept of Meter," p. 587.

33  William Beare, *Latin Verse and European Song: A Study in Accent and Rhythm* (London: Methuen, 1957), pp. 15–19.

34  The term *versus* originally referred to the turn that the ploughman made at the end of one furrow before beginning a new one. See Beare, p. 20.

CHAPTER TWO

1  WCW, "Seafarer," *Interim* 3, no. 3 (1948): 20.

2  Jan Tschichold, *Asymmetric Typography*, trans. Ruari Mclean (New York: Reinhold Publishing Corporation, 1967), p. 48.

3  Tschichold, p. 20.

4  *The Poetical Works of Wordsworth*, ed. Thomas Hutchinson, rev. Ernest

de Selincourt (London and New York: Oxford University Press, 1965), p. 702.

5   When Keats is at his most Miltonic in *Hyperion* and *Fall of Hyperion*, he uses the verse paragraph as Milton does.

6   WCW, *I Wanted to Write a Poem*, ed. Edith Heal, rev. ed. (Boston: Beacon Press, 1967), p. 36.

7   WCW, *Imaginations*, pp. 96, 115.

8   WCW, "Rome," ed. Steven Ross Loevy, *Iowa Review* 9, no. 3 (Summer 1978): 59. The syntactic and grammatical oddities are Williams's own.

9   Cummings, *Complete Poems*, pp. 396, 673. The motions of a grasshopper are suggested by various permutations of the letters of "grasshopper" and other typographical gestures:

                    r-p-o-p-h-e-s-s-a-g-r

              who

a)s w(e loo)k
upnowgath
            PPEGORHRASS
                            eringint(o-
aThe):l
         eA
            !p:
S                                        a
              (r
rIvInG
                    .gRrEaPsPhOs)
                            to
rea(be)rran(com)gi(e)ngly
,grasshopper;

Typographic jumbling, dispersion, rearrangement, and, finally, stability enact the transformation of the motionless grasshopper into a leaping blur of energy, which suddenly comes to rest. The poem also dramatizes the act of looking at the grasshopper and not realizing what it is (the grasshopper may be camouflaged in the grass as the word "grasshopper" is camouflaged in the first line) until it leaps into the air and into attention and recognition.

10  Hartman, pp. 12–13.

11  William K. Wimsatt, Jr., *Day of the Leopards: Essays in Defense of Poems* (New Haven and London: Yale University Press, 1976), p. 72.

12  John Sparrow, *Visible Words: A Study of Inscriptions in and as Books and Works of Art* (Cambridge: Cambridge University Press, 1969), p. 4.

13  WCW, Poetry and Rare Books Collection, State University of New York at Buffalo, New York, C145, TS, n.p.

14  Linda Welshimer Wagner, *The Poems of William Carlos Williams: A Critical Study* (Middletown, Connecticut: Wesleyan University Press, 1964), p. 81.

15  WCW, "Measure," p. 149.

16  "Introduction" to *Concrete Poetry: A World View*, ed. Mary Ellen Solt (Bloomington, Indiana: Indiana University Press, 1968), p. 53.

17  In addition to Henry Sayre's *The Visual Text of William Carlos Williams*, mentioned in the Introduction, see Bram Dijkstra, *Cubism, Stieglitz, and the Early Poetry of William Carlos Williams: The Hieroglyphics of a New Speech* (Princeton, New Jersey: Princeton University Press, 1969); Dikran Tashjian, *Skyscraper Primitives: Dada and the American Avant-Garde, 1910–1925* (Middletown, Connecticut: Wesleyan University Press, 1975) and *William Carlos Williams and the American Scene* (Berkeley and Los Angeles: University of California Press, 1982); William Marling, *William Carlos Williams and the Painters, 1909–1923* (Athens, Ohio: Ohio University Press, 1982). See also Peter Schmidt, "Some Versions of Modernist Pastoral: Williams and the Precisionists," *Contemporary Literature* 21 (Summer 1980): 383–406; Henry Sayre, "The Tyranny of the Image: The Aesthetic Background," *William Carlos Williams Review* 9, nos. 1–2 (Fall 1983): 125–34; and Wallace, "The Satyrs' Abstract and Chronicle," 136–55.

18  Reed Whittemore, *William Carlos Williams: Poet from New Jersey* (Boston: Houghton Mifflin, 1975), p. 118.

19  Cummings, p. 541.

20  *A Recognizable Image: William Carlos Williams on Art and Artists*, ed. Bram Dijkstra (New York: New Directions, 1978), p. 236.

21  Mary Ellen Solt sees in many of Williams's poems "strong impulses towards concretization," as in the river passage of *Paterson*, Book Three, in which the lines slant in several directions (*Concrete Poetry*, p. 48). Defining concrete poetry is beyond the scope of this book. Some so-called concrete poems seem to be acts of mimetic representation; others tend toward more abstract designs. Hollander's rule of thumb is a useful guide: "Since a true concrete poem cannot be read aloud, it has no full linguistic dimension, no existence in the ear's kingdom" (Hollander, *Vision and Resonance*, p. 266). The poems I am concerned with here do exist in the ear's kingdom, as well as the eye's.

22  Tschichold, p. 58.

23  Tschichold, p. 59.

24  Tschichold, p. 84.

25  Charles Hartman defines verse as "language in lines" (*Free Verse*, p. 11).

26  Ernest Fenollosa, *The Chinese Written Character as a Medium for Poetry*, ed. Ezra Pound (San Francisco: City Lights Books, 1936), p. 8. Today scholars of Chinese do not accept this view.

27 Sparrow, p. 5.
28 Sparrow, pp. 2–3.
29 For a discussion of Williams's revisions through subsequent stages of a single poem, see my article "Williams Revising: The Worksheets of 'Threnody,' " *William Carlos Williams Review* 8, no. 2 (Fall 1982): 23–28.
30 WCW, *I Wanted to Write a Poem*, p. 76.
31 WCW, *I Wanted to Write a Poem*, p. 76.
32 WCW, Poetry and Rare Books Collection, SUNY at Buffalo, A53(f).
33 Letter to Weaver, 11 February 1966; quoted by Weaver, *The American Background*, pp. 85–86; compare Hugh Kenner, *The Pound Era* (Berkeley and Los Angeles: University of California Press, 1971), p. 541.
34 Weaver, p. 85.
35 Weaver, p. 86.
36 WCW, *Selected Letters*, pp. 325–27.
37 Hartman, p. 35; Emma Mellard Kafalenos, "Possibilities of Isochrony" (Ph.D. diss., Washington University, 1974).
38 Hartman, p. 66.
39 Hartman, p. 36.
40 Recently Mariani and Solt have followed Williams down the quantitative path. See Mariani, *A New World Naked*, pp. 539, 690; and Solt, "The American Idiom," *William Carlos Williams Review* 9, nos. 1–2 (Fall 1983): 111–20.
41 *The Complete Stories and Poems of Edgar Allan Poe*, II, 1005.
42 See John C. Thirlwall, "The Lost Poems of William Carlos Williams," *New Directions 16* (1957), pp. 44–45; also Thirlwall's "Ten Years of a New Rhythm," *Pictures from Brueghel*, p. 183.
43 See, for example, "A Retrospective," "The Tradition," and "Vers Libre and Arnold Dolmetsch," in *The Literary Essays of Ezra Pound* (Norfolk, Connecticut: New Directions, 1954), pp. 12–13, 90–91, 437–40.
44 Hartman, p. 17.
45 Wagner, *The Poems of William Carlos Williams*, p. 93.
46 Hartman, p. 17.
47 WCW, *Selected Essays*, p. 206.
48 Jerrald Ranta, "William Carlos Williams' Prosody to 1940" (Ph.D. diss., Kent State University, 1968), pp. 137 ff.
49 WCW, *I Wanted to Write a Poem*, pp. 65–66.
50 Rudolph Arnheim, *Art and Visual Perception: A Psychology of the Creative Eye*, rev. ed. (Berkeley and Los Angeles: University of California Press, 1974), p. 34.
51 For a further discussion of "descent" in Williams's poetry, both as explicit theme and implicit pattern, see Thomas R. Whitaker, *William Carlos Williams* (Boston: Twayne Publishers, 1968), passim.
52 See *Vision and Resonance*, pp. 236–42, for Hollander's persuasive sug-

gestion that Williams's triadic format derived from Pound's printing of Cavalcanti's *Donna mi Prega* ("Cavalcanti," *Literary Essays*, pp. 163–67).
53  Letter to Cid Corman, 30 November 1955; quoted by Mariani, p. 689.


CHAPTER THREE

1  Letter to Burke, 24 January 1951; quoted by Mariani, p. 633.
2  Samuel Taylor Coleridge, "On Poesy or Art," printed in *Biographia Literaria*, ed. John Shawcross (New York: Oxford University Press, 1965), II, 265.
3  Mariani, p. 400.
4  *Aristotle's Poetics*, trans. S. H. Butcher, intro. Francis Fergusson (New York: Hill and Wang, 1961), p. 108.
5  Emily Mitchell Wallace, "A Musing in the Highlands and Valleys: The Poetry of Gratwick Farm," *William Carlos Williams Review* 8, no. 1 (Spring 1982): 27.
6  WCW, "Measure," p. 156.
7  Barbara Herrnstein Smith, *Poetic Closure: A Study of How Poems End* (Chicago: University of Chicago Press, 1968), p. 15.
8  For the view that there is something enjambment-like in the way Americans speak, see Hugh Kenner, "The Rhythm of Ideas," *New York Times Book Review* (September 18, 1983).
9  WCW, *Paterson*, pp. 122, 130.
10  WCW, *Selected Letters*, pp. 315–16.
11  WCW, "VS," *Touchstone* 1, no. 3 (January 1948): 1–4; these passages quoted by Ranta, p. 42.
12  WCW, *Selected Essays*, pp. 204–05, 207.
13  Daniel Hoffman, "Poetry: After Modernism" in *Harvard Guide to Contemporary American Writing*, ed. Daniel Hoffman (Cambridge, Mass. and London: Belknap Press, 1979), p. 460.
14  *Aristotle's Poetics*, p. 109.
15  See M. H. Abrams, *The Mirror and the Lamp: Romantic Theory and the Critical Tradition* (New York: Oxford University Press, 1953), especially chapter one; or see Abrams's entry "Poetry, Theories of" in *Princeton Encyclopedia of Poetry and Poetics*.
16  A modified version of a formulation by Harvey Gross in "The Phenomenology of Rhythm," *The Structure of Verse: Modern Essays on Prosody*, ed. Harvey Gross, rev. ed. (New York: Ecco Press, 1979), p. 14.
17  WCW, quoted by Mariani, p. 497.
18  WCW, *Autobiography*, pp. 332–33.
19  WCW, quoted by Mariani, p. 682.
20  Denise Levertov, *The Poet in the World* (New York: New Directions, 1973), p. 257.

21  Compare Williams's earlier discussions of Juan Gris's version of Cubism in *A Novelette* (*I*, pp. 283–89) and *Spring and All* (*I*, pp. 107, 110–11). See also Sayre, *The Visual Text*, pp. 31–33, 43–44. The "Without invention" passage enacts Williams's principle of "conversation as design," as it selects diverse objects or details and arranges them in a unified design.

22  WCW, *Selected Letters*, p. 331.

23  WCW, *Selected Letters*, p. 331.

24  *Aristotle's Poetics*, p. 57; see also Fergusson's introduction, p. 37.

25  WCW, *Selected Letters*, p. 336.

26  WCW, *Selected Essays*, p. 340.

27  WCW, "Measure," p. 154.

28  WCW, "Let Us Order Our World," with an introduction by Augustus M. Kolich, *William Carlos Williams Review* 8, no. 2 (Fall 1982): 17.

29  WCW, "Let Us Order Our World."

30  Mariani, p. 516.

31  WCW, *Selected Essays*, pp. 187–88.

32  Ezra Pound, *The Cantos of Ezra Pound* (New York: New Directions, 1972), p. 59.

33  WCW, *Selected Essays*, p. 109.

34  Ezra Pound, *Jefferson and/or Mussolini: L'Idea Statale: Fascism As I Have Seen It* (London: Stanley Nott, 1935), p. 99.

35  Louis L. Martz juxtaposes these passages (*Cantos*, pp. 229–30) with the *Paterson* passage in his essay "The Unicorn in *Paterson*: William Carlos Williams," *Thought: A Review of Culture and Idea* 35 (Winter 1960): 548–49; repr. in *William Carlos Williams: A Collection of Critical Essays*, ed. J. Hillis Miller (Englewood Cliffs, N.J.: Prentice-Hall, 1966), pp. 70–87. The suggestion that Pound is adopting the manner of a preacher is Martz's.

36  Mariani, p. 476.

37  T. S. Eliot, "The Music of Poetry," *On Poetry and Poets* (New York: Farrar, Straus, and Giroux, 1957), pp. 21, 28, 24, 25, 29.

38  T. S. Eliot, "Reflections on *Vers Libre*"; repr. in Gross, *The Structure of Verse*, pp. 230–32.

39  WCW, *Selected Letters*, p. 335.

40  Mariani, pp. 12, 609.

41  For Tapscott's comments on Williams and Emerson, as well as his summary of earlier discussions, see *American Beauty*, pp. 90–91, 237n, 246–47n. Contending that the argument of "The Red Wheelbarrow" is "Emersonian," Tapscott qualifies this assertion, explaining that he does not want to designate "strict literary-historical antecedents for Williams' sense of wonder": "Even the adjective 'Emersonian' here presupposes a literary precedent I do not mean to claim too strongly." Instead, Tapscott claims that what Williams did learn from "the Emerson-Whitman model" is "the association between such personal verve and the universality of local detail" (p. 90). This claim is persuasive,

and the qualification careful and responsible. But Tapscott is too tentative here. In another recent study, Carl Rapp devotes an entire chapter to "Emerson the Precursor" [*William Carlos Williams and Romantic Idealism* (Hanover and London: University Press of New England, 1984), pp. 55–77]. Demonstrating "Williams' Emersonian habits of interpretation," Rapp makes this bold claim: "In America no one has wrestled with this problem [of symbols] more conspicuously than Emerson, which probably explains why Emerson, more than any other writer, provides a key to Williams" (p. 55). With the phrase "more than any other writer," Rapp may be overestimating the relationship Tapscott underestimates; yet he rightly calls attention to its significance.

42  *Journals of Ralph Waldo Emerson*, ed. Edward W. Emerson (Cambridge, Mass.: Riverside Press, 1909–1914), X, 166.

# Index

Grateful acknowledgment is given to: